MEMOIRS OF A WORLD WAR TWO ROYAL ENGINEER

Harry Ivor Dunstan

6th Airborne Division
3rd Parachute Squadron RE

Dunestone Publishing ®
available at Amazon.com and other book stores

Copyright © 07/07/2015 by Peter Dunstan

All rights reserved. No part of this book may be reproduced, stored in a retrieval system, or transferred by any other means, electronic, mechanical, photocopying, recording or otherwise, without written permission of the author.

These memoirs were transcribed and edited by Peter Dunstan from hand-written letters, assorted notes and digital files stored on a floppy disk by his father:
Harry Ivor Dunstan, 1920 – 2004.

A Dunestone Publishing ® book
Author email: pd_designer@yahoo.com

Printed by CreateSpace, an Amazon.com company
_____

Library of Congress Cataloging-in-Publication Data

Dunstan, Peter
   Memoirs Of A World War Two Royal Engineer.

ISBN-13: 9781515146254   ISBN-10: 1515146251

   1. Non-Fiction -- History -- Europe -- General
   2. Non-Fiction -- History -- Modern -- 20th C
I.Title.

10   9   8   7   6   5

III

Harry Ivor Dunstan - 1943

IV

CONTENTS

THE APPRENTICE IN TRAINING 1

CHEPSTOW & THE BOYS TECHNICAL SCHOOL AT BEACHLEY 1
THE FINAL YEAR AT BEACHLEY 43
CHATHAM 48
ALDERSHOT 55

THE PHONEY WAR & DUNKIRK 63

CHAPTER 1 63
CHAPTER 2 87

D-DAY: INTO ACTION BY AIR 107

ABOUT THE ENGINEER 152

VI

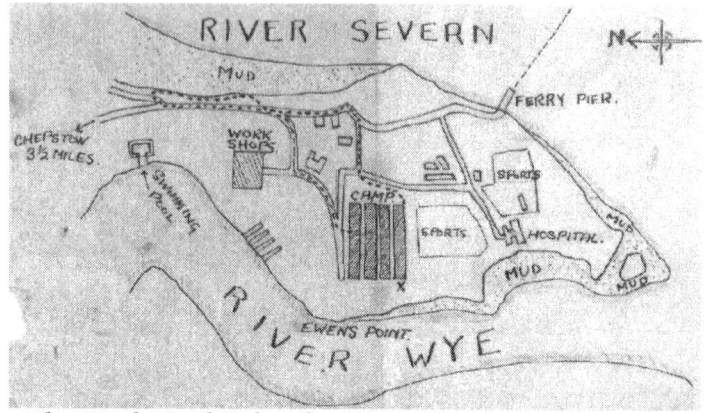

The Technical School at Beachley near Chepstow
sketch - from a letter to his parents - 1935

The Apprentice in Training - 1936

The Apprentice in Training

Chepstow & The Boys Technical School At Beachley

The tide drives a wedge of water up the Bristol Channel between the ever-narrowing coasts: Wales on one side, Somerset on the other, until at the Severn estuary the water is forty feet higher. A few minutes later the tide has turned and this incredible volume of water - scores of square miles and forty feet deep - runs out again, leaving only a mixture of salt and fresh river water to meander between vast areas of fine squelchy mud. At this estuary, where the smaller River Wye joins the Severn, is a peninsula with its small village of Beachley. A ferry plies between the village and Aust, two miles away in Gloucestershire. Traffic arriving from England can then reach Wales by using a bridge at Chepstow three miles away.

Here maximum spring tides, the second highest in the world, can be up to forty-seven feet and even higher, and occur around 21st March and 21st September. These bring about the Severn Bore, when the change in water level forms a fast moving wave that starts near Beachley and follows the Severn northwards until it peters out.

Far bigger than the village is the army camp, originally built during World War I as a prisoner-of-war camp, followed by an abortive attempt to build naval ships to be launched into the Wye, and then from 1925 extended and used as a school for training boys to be army tradesmen.

On January 16th 1935 I found my way to Chepstow railway station via Plymouth and Bristol, and then an eerie seven-mile ride alone in a compartment through the Severn Tunnel. It was the first time I had been north of Plymouth. There were several other boys on the platform in Chepstow, gathered in the rain, so I joined them. A soldier, an adult, shepherded us on to a covered truck with benches inside, and we departed for BTS (the Boys Technical School) beside Beachley village on the peninsula. I was to discover that the soldier, Private Carey RASC (Royal Army Service Corps), drove the only truck in the school.

We dismounted with our suitcases and entered a white building with a clock tower. Inside, each of us was given a card with his name on it, and a number, mine being 2680. We were then taken to our various barrack rooms, now nearly full, and the boys in mine were getting ready for bed. We were told the time of 'lights out' and 'reveille', the time of the breakfast parade, and the names of the boy corporal and adult sergeant who would be responsible for us. There wasn't much time before 'lights out', and there was little chatter. The bed was heavy iron, one half sliding below the other, and the mattress was made up of three square cushions about thirty inches across and packed with horse-hair, called "biscuits". The bolster was also stuffed with horsehair. The hard grey stiff sheets smelled of soap, and on them were two blankets. I climbed into bed and settled as a bugle sounded and the lights were extinguished. I was warm - there was a brick tower in the centre of the room with a banked down coal fire on each side of it. The bed was hard, but I felt okay.

In the morning a boy corporal woke us, and we soon washed in the adjoining annex. We folded and tidied our bedding and assembled outside, and then walked single-file on a road leading north to two large dining halls with a cookhouse between. There were eight hundred boys in these dining halls - all sitting at tables arranged in lines of three, with two more placed at right angles at one end and used for serving the food. We had porridge, bread and margarine, meat and potato rissoles, and a pint of sweet tea. We then walked individually back to the barrack room.

On our first day we were taught the rudiments of military drill. That is, we were arranged in two lines, one behind the other. We were taught to turn to the left or right, to march, and to halt, and to disperse on the order, "Dismiss." This then enabled an NCO (Non Commissioned Officer) to start teaching us the finer points. At first nobody seemed to like drill. It was only later, much later, that we started to appreciate its purpose, to realize that it was a smart and quick way of moving a compact unit of soldiers from one place to another, based on the principle of immediate and unquestioning response to short commands, and on men being alert and proud of their appearance.

On the first visit to the quartermaster's store we were issued with chocolate coloured overalls for working in, the material being almost as stiff as a cardboard box. We were soon to discover that these overalls rapidly softened in the wash and bleached to a pale mushroom colour. Khaki serge tunic and trousers were issued for school wear and for parades. Both overalls and serge were fitted oversize initially, to allow for growth, and nobody looked happy about this. Then, coarse khaki shirts, unbleached underpants, long and short, and two pairs of grey socks. Also heavy leather boots and light canvas gym shoes, and khaki drill gym shorts. Then a 'housewife' - a strange little cotton wallet containing a skein of grey wool, cotton thread and a set of needles. Also a pair of puttees, a waterproof ground sheet and a heavy greatcoat. A peaked cap was issued, and a forage cap, together with a general service cap badge (the lion and unicorn), plus the BTS epaulette insignia. And finally, we received plenty of brown paper and string and instructions to make a parcel of our civilian clothes that would be posted home.

It was then that we were told our mailing address. It was The Boys Technical School, Chepstow, Monmouthshire. It was much later that I discovered that the school was actually in Gloucestershire, England. That is, it was east of the River Wye, whereas Chepstow was west of the river, and in Wales. Nevertheless, in the army we were known as Chepstow boys.

We started getting to know our colleagues. A serious looking boy called Garwood, an electrician-to-be like myself, looked very observant and steady. A muscular boy called Moore was going to be a blacksmith, and so was tall red-haired Greenwood; they were both from the Isle of Wight. Another boy, Roots, also a future electrician, took several opportunities to talk to me, and we started to team up together.

We soon discovered that at this time the school was divided into three companies according to trades. Electricians and instrument repairers were together in the same company as the smiths (blacksmiths, coppersmiths and tinsmiths). Fitters and turners were in another company. And so were masons, bricklayers, and painters. It was some time later that the smiths were formed into a separate company from the electricians and instrument repairers, so we no longer shared barrack rooms with them.

Besides Moore and Greenwood there was also a blacksmith called Sadd, the son of a serving sergeant, who was soon called Snowy because of his light blond hair. Snowy Sadd was bursting with good humour, and it was a pleasure to live in the same barrack room as him. There was also Pegg from Newcastle. I got to know him quite early because he and I and another electrician called Addison were in the small group of Methodists for church service on Sundays. It was some time before I could understand Pegg because of his strong Geordie (Newcastle) accent.

A boy called Johnston was another blacksmith. He was the son of an ex-serviceman who kept a pub in Farnham, Surrey. He was a very likeable chap, a real character who often liked to burst into song or to tell a story. Among the other electrical apprentices there were Sturge, Naunton, Fordham, Shearman, Roots and Ballard, all tall, friendly and likable. I was soon to meet other electricians; Bolton, Shiel, Cartlidge, Butler, Going, Hill, Hampton, Elliott, Bryan, Watkinson, Cockle and Slater, a total of twenty-one electricians and four instrument mechanics that I would get to know very well during the next three years. The various smiths mentioned would be transferred to the re-formed 'A' Company and we would see less of them.

Barrack rooms were in blocks of four 'H' blocks where the connecting 'bar' was an annex with toilets and washbasins (cold water only). In each room there were usually sixteen beds, each with a shelf on the wall behind, and in the centre of the room a square brick tower, occasionally called the Cenotaph, with a fireplace and hearth on two sides of it. Each room was provided with a heavy steel coal bunker, a coal bucket, a galvanized bucket, two sweeping brushes, a wooden table top with heavy iron trestles, two wooden benches, and a bumper, the bumper being a weighted stiff brush on the end of a handle and used for polishing floors. All these items were arranged in a certain pattern. The table with the benches being placed centrally in the room, the coal bucket hung from a table trestle, and next to it the galvanized bucket. Then the bumper with a brush each side, all radiating down to a point.

The centre line of all this followed the centre line of the gleaming jarrah hardwood floor. The table and forms were scrubbed white, as were the broom handles, and the steel table corners were shining after thorough cleaning with emery cloth. The hearths were evenly coated with hearthstone. Behind each bed, made up to so-called 'arm chair fashion', was a shelf with the boy's service cap placed centrally, a drinking mug on one side and a dental mug on the other. Below this, again placed centrally, was his haversack, with the straps spread to hang from two pegs. From one peg hung the rolled greatcoat, and from the other a rubberized fabric ground sheet, also rolled. In addition there were his two belts: a three-inch wide webbing belt and a two-inch wide white leather belt. In front of each bed was the boy's kit box, about thirty by fifteen inches by a foot deep, fitted with hasp and staple suitable for adding a padlock. On it were his best boots with gym shoes either side.

Such a barrack room, shining and ready for inspection, was the most uncomfortable place ever devised. It was cleaned to this standard every day before the boys left for parades or work. It was in the evenings or on weekends, when the beds were made down, that the rooms became more comfortable. Most rooms had one corner partitioned off and used as accommodation for an NCO, either a wing sergeant or a boy NCO.

Soon our training in military drill - "square bashing" - started in earnest, and continued for several weeks under a sergeant called Logan, interrupted only for a daily one hour session in the gymnasium and occasional lectures, and for a cross country run every month, and of course for a bath parade. The bath-house was sandwiched between rows of barrack blocks, and attended by an ex-service man. Each bath was a concrete 'tub' where a boy could sit in water up to a foot deep, the tubs being ranged along each of the long walls of the building, and between them were benches and a screen with pegs where we could undress. Bath day was most enjoyable, the crowd of naked boys all leaping into the concrete 'tubs' in a long room full of steam, and often singing, a favourite song being "Old Faithful".

Old Faithful, we roam the range together
Old Faithful, in any kind of weather
When your round-up days are over
There'll be pastures white with clover
For you, old faithful pal of mine.

We were marched to the bath-house and of course marched back to our barrack blocks afterward, clean and usually cheerful.

The simplest form of drill was firstly to 'Fall in' and on this command the boys quickly assembled in two lines: the first line (usually nearest any sidewalk) with the boys standing shoulder to shoulder, close but not touching, and the second line immediately behind. The squad commander then gave the orders, "Move to the right (or left) in file. Right turn - Quick march!" And at the destination, "Halt!" and then, "Fall out," upon which the boys dispersed.

Being young, we new recruits learned quickly. We were soon standing ram-rod straight, with shoulders braced back, each arm a straight line from shoulder to thumb. Soon it was automatic to feel for the seam of the trousers with the thumb. One held one's head erect with the chin neatly pulled in, and the eyes looking ahead and slightly up. The stomach was firmly pulled in, the knees braced back, heels together and the feet at forty-five degrees.

When marching a pace was thirty inches long, and one quickly learned to ensure that one's feet fell exactly together with the rest. CSM (Company Sergeant Major) Slee of the Cameronians appeared on the parade ground for a brief visit on most days, invariably dressed in a kilt, cutaway tunic and glengarry, and white spats - stern and smart as paint. He was dedicated in his drill commands, quick and precise. If he found us drilling on gravel he moved us to a tarmac surface where the sound of our marching was clipped and precise. Far from being a bully, he was an enthusiast. But most of the drill was under Sergeant Logan, the drill sergeant, a serious instructor who schooled us thoroughly.

If a boy received a command "Right turn" he turned his right foot by keeping his right heel on the ground while turning his toe clockwise, and simultaneously keeping the ball of his left foot on the ground while turning his left heel clockwise. Meanwhile his body was turned to the right. The movement was completed by bringing his left foot forward to its normal position next to the right foot. The command "Left turn" initiated similar but opposite movements.

As we learned these movements so others were added, depending on the need and the circumstances. Most movements were in fours; that is, the boys would be marched along a road four abreast. On a church parade or other formal parade boys were graded according to height, the taller ones being at the ends of a column, grading down to the shorter ones in the centre of that column. We learned the precise way of achieving this:

1. First command: "Tallest on the right, shortest on the left, in single rank SIZE." You soon learned your positions. You just walked along until you were with boys of similar height, and then got into line.

2. "Number One, stand fast. Even numbers one pace forward, odd numbers one pace step-back MARCH."

3. "Ranks, right and left TURN." Number One remains stationary. The even numbers that are in front turn right, and the odd numbers who are in the rear turn left.

4. "QUICK MARCH!"

Number 1 still remains stationary. Number 2 takes his position behind him, thereby starting the new rear rank. Then Number 3 joins No 1 in the front rank - and so it continues. Each man turns to his left (i.e. the front) on arrival. The squad will now be in two ranks with the tallest at the ends and the shortest in the centre. The system of 'sizing' troops ensured that a tall person never stood beside a short person, but was not used except for formal parades. When it was used it did tend to make a number of troops appear to be of the same height. We were taught many other drill manoeuvres before our 'square-bashing' was finished, and then started trade training, which was almost continuous except for classroom studies, visits to the gymnasium and the occasional cross-country run.

The higher ground in the centre of Beachley was occupied by the barrack blocks, dining rooms, the school church, classrooms and company offices, with the numerous playing fields extending southwards and separated from the rivers (the Severn and the Wye) by a narrow plantation of small conifers. The barrack rooms where I and the other electricians were quartered was in the nearest corner to the Wye, and gave easy access to a path round most of the south and west sides of the outer perimeter of the school grounds, a pleasant walk. The officer and NCO married quarters were along the east side, and a civilian church, also the slipway for the Severn ferry with a small teashop nearby. North of this was an area of lower ground occupied by the extensive workshops and the main administrative block dominated by a clock tower, the same block where we had been received on arrival. Near these workshops were a number of disused slipways on the bank of the River Wye.

After our first cross-country run we had a good idea of the whole camp layout. Starting from our block, which was at the southeast corner of all the blocks, we would run on the road going east, with the playing field area and its numerous football pitches spread out on our right. We then headed northeast for the gym and then swung into the main road leading northwards towards Chepstow. This was where we struggled to get our second wind, gasping and breathless, but no one wanted to be last. Less than a mile later we left the road and descended a path angled down the cliff to the Severn foreshore where there was a fine view of the broad river spreading about two miles to the brick coloured cliffs at Aust on the far side, or mostly of mud if the tide was out. Another mile or more and we left the river to climb again and cross the road once more past some houses called "The Three Salmons."

Then to the east with the Wye ahead of us, about three hundred yards of water, or mud if the tide was out, and we were running through fields with the swimming pool below us and the workshops far to our left. We swung to the left and made our way to the camp following the road that passed through the workshops, past the white administration block, and finally climbed the slope to the barrack blocks.

After those initial weeks of drill, or 'square bashing', we were paraded in overalls and forage caps and marched to the workshops to start trade training, which began with a few weeks when we were schooled in the use of hand tools. Day after day we stood at a bench hammering at a piece of steel, six inches square and three quarters of an inch thick, with another piece just over two inches square. The task was to cut a hole exactly two inches square in the larger piece, and then to reduce the smaller piece to the same size as the hole. The standard of the work was determined by using feeler gauges to assess how well the small piece fitted into the larger piece, and of course it could be fitted four ways, and then turned over and fitted a further four ways. We then repeated the task with other shapes. The tools we had were essentially a ball pane hammer, various chisels, a square and a steel rule, and a hacksaw, plus various files. We also had access to various other tools such as micrometers. At the end of this exercise the boys selected as suitable for training as instrument mechanics were chosen. I was now able to wield a one-pound hammer accurately and with confidence, holding it by the end of the handle and putting maximum effort into the job, and watching the chisel closely throughout while a shaving of steel curled away.

It was now that we started the real training as electricians, and the instrument mechanics - Tim Egan, Jimmie Neeve, Humphreys and Pete Moyser - started their training, which was similar to ours in some ways, and specialized in others. We learned the nature of electricity, Ohm's Law, metals and materials used as conductors and insulators, simple wiring circuits, the Wheatstone bridge, static electricity and the Wimshurst machine. During one lecture by Mr. Milliner (nicknamed 'Pesky'), a boy was invited to stand on a stool with insulated legs, and to hold one conductor while the other was held over his head, with Mr. Milliner turning the handle of the Wimshurst machine. Strands of the boy's hair started to reach up towards that second conductor, which was then moved near the boy's nose, whereupon a spark jumped off his nose with a loud crack! The class roared with laughter while a surprised but unharmed boy went back to his seat. Few lectures were so amusing, but were informative and interesting, and were usually written up in our fair notebooks, fat quarto sized army issue.

Each morning we had a short break, when we wandered around talking, or sometimes climbing the few trees nearby. We were also given a drink of skimmed milk. Maybe ten per cent of the boys smoked - a pastime that of course was forbidden - and the smokers congregated in the outside toilets. It was impossible to use a toilet at this time; in fact it was most difficult to enter. Two boys would share each toilet seat, and four more would sit on their knees, and in addition all standing room was occupied. A few would be smoking whole cigarettes, most had butt ends, and a few were there scrounging, with such remarks as, "After you Joe," or "After you Bill with the 'angings,'" and even, "After you with the supers," meaning the super-hangings or very last scraps, which were invariably so small that they were held between two match-stick ends and sucked very carefully.

These toilets were enclosed by brick walls but were open to the air, and were only fifty yards or less from where the instructors squatted with their pipes and cigarettes. The blue haze that came from the toilet enclosure was obvious to anyone, but we only heard of one action being taken against the smokers, and that was by Sergeant Reynolds of the RASC who thereby earned himself the nickname 'Smokey'. But in the barrack blocks smokers were always getting caught and 'put on a charge', when they were punished. A smoker would often be surprised by a sudden visit from a wing sergeant.

In the winter evenings, boys would often be seen with their faces uncomfortably near the fire as they attempted to puff their smoke up the chimney. An unusual method of producing a light was to soak a small piece of paper in metal polish. Then two pieces of pencil, sharpened at both ends, were used to hold the paper between them while the other ends were pressed against the terminals inside an electric light switch - the switch cover having been removed. By jiggling the pencils, sparks would result and the metal polish on the paper would be ignited. Sometimes the lights would be fused. When one saw that the lights in a room were flickering it usually meant that someone was lighting a 'cig'. To obtain cigarettes one had to go to Chepstow and buy them, or, if some relative or friend was willing, get them sent in a food parcel by post. This was risky, as all parcels were inspected and concealment of cigarettes was difficult. I knew of instances where cigarettes were successfully hidden in a cake. Usually the packet was fitted into a hole and the hole covered with a sliver of cake.

It was about this time back at the barracks that I had my first brush with a boy NCO. His name was Gasky, and he had (to me) a very noticeable way of marching. It was usual for one's arm to reach its maximum swing forward as the opposite heel hit the ground. While a whole troop was doing this Gasky's arm had already swung back to the vertical position - that is, his arm went down when all the rest were going forward. Many boys had noticed it and guffawed, but not in his hearing. My face must have shown surprise, because later he stopped me on the way to the mess hall and berated me for not standing to attention while he was addressing me. I protested, so he told me not to answer back, and to double to a tree about seventy paces away. My running was not to his liking, so I had to do it again before he let me go, with a warning to behave in future. As I marched smartly away I fumed and wondered if I should report him. I knew reporting him would be most serious. It was just not done to report such incidents, as all senior boys would be watching me thereafter. So I did nothing.

Meantime Slater (mischievously nicknamed 'Oscar' after a murderer currently in the news) had upset some senior boy. Oscar was a nice chap, but was so painfully shy that he could hardly speak to anyone. Nobody knew the reason but he was dragged off one night blindfolded to a roomful of seniors and subjected to a 'court martial'. He couldn't remember half of what they trumped up against him, but the 'president' decreed that he was guilty. Thereupon they forced his head into a kitbag and suspended him - upside down - from a beam in the ceiling and danced around him whacking him with walking-out canes. Then the rope broke, and he fell head first to the floor. The seniors, in a panic, got the kit bag off him and found him shaken but otherwise okay, so they took him to his barrack room and left him there - outside - in the dark. Oscar took a while to tell anyone what had happened, and refused to report the incident.

But such incidents were rare, and possibly arose because of boredom. Much later I was reminded of those happenings when a boy called Haynes, junior to us, was bullied. Haynes had an educated accent, which alone was enough to provoke some teasing, simply because he was different. He could also quickly and expertly write in shorthand. He would ask if anyone wanted anything at the NAAFI (the Navy Army Air Force Institute which provided goods and services to the armed forces) and would write down the items in shorthand. Many of the boys found this mind boggling, and would make sarcastic remarks about it. But on one occasion Haynes was standing outside the ablutions being dowsed with buckets of water by boys from my own group. Then the gang took him inside a barrack room and forced him to the floor with his nose close to an eraser on a joint in the floorboards. I came in with two others and we asked what he had done. Our questions were ignored as they surrounded him with raised walking-out canes, warning him that he must push the eraser to the end of the room, and if his nose left the eraser or the eraser left the floor joint he was going to get a whack. He got a whack to the accompanying yells of his tormentors, and he leaped to his feet with an agonized howl and bolted through the door and sprinted towards the river bawling, "I won't take this - I'd rather drown!" I joined the boys pursuing him and suddenly he was in the centre of a group who were saying, "It's all right Haynes," and trying hard to pacify him. He was sitting in the centre, shaking and staring at the ground white-faced. After a while he calmed down and a small group stayed with him. The incident was discussed and argued over for some time, most of us realizing how shameful our behaviour had been.

Shortly after this we were on the receiving end. A senior boy seemed to imagine that a boy from my barrack room was 'lacking in suitable respect' and warned him that he would be "raided" soon. It was late spring and quite warm, and that night we went to sleep with the windows closed. The next night we went to bed but within half an hour some boys were complaining of the heat and opened a window. There was silence for a while and then - within thirty seconds - the raiders had come and gone. The first raider came through that window like a fast moving shadow - he then ran to the door and quickly removed the broom handles that had been jammed through the door handle. Two boys then ran in, jumping from bed to bed on the sleeping occupants and sweeping everything from shelves with a walking stick as they jumped. Amid the noise of breaking mugs the next pair ran through, tipping each bed so that the lower half of each bed was folded over the sleeper. Meanwhile coal from the bunker was shovelled into buckets and then coal and water was flung over everyone. Then they were gone. All that for some imagined slight! It took us two hours to clean up.

Most winter evenings were spent yarning, reading or listening to the wireless, as the radio was called. Papers and magazines were passed around and their contents discussed. We all gathered around the fireplace to hear the serial "Sweeny Todd the Demon Barber" on George Garwood's wireless. Butler had his own set too, which he tuned in to short-wave stations worldwide. He corresponded with numerous broadcasters, many of whom sent him their call station cards, so he applied for and got permission to pin these cards on the wall - scores of them.

Then of course there were some who spent time 'blancoing' their equipment or boning their boots.

The term 'blanco' applied to the blocks that were wetted and the colour applied to our equipment. I suppose the stuff used for white belts was originally called 'blanco', but the name came to apply to the khaki colour as well. 'Boning' was a method of polishing boots. After the polish was liberally applied using a cloth, the surface was rapidly rubbed with a toothbrush handle, which built up a glaze of hard polish. Spit was also applied during boning - hence 'spit and polish'.

We often brewed tea in the winter evenings, and many of us made a small bag out of cotton fabric, with draw string attached, to hold the tea leaves in the boiling water. In spite of regular washing the bags soon became almost black, but they usually continued in use until they disintegrated. We also made toast. I was stopped when leaving the mess room by a sergeant who wanted to know what was in the suspicious bulge in my trousers. Having discovered the bread that was there, he confiscated it and instructed me to report to the company office next morning at 9am. "And put on clean fatigues," he said, meaning best serge without puttees or white belt. Next morning I was marched in to the company office by CSM Slee and halted, hatless, before the company commander, Captain Kennedy, who, with his florid face bulging over his collar, stared at me while the charge was read out. He questioned me and I admitted the charge, whereupon he said, "Four days CB. March him out, Sergeant Major." Outside, the sergeant major barked "To the guard room, double march," and I duly ran to the guardroom and joined two other boys from other companies who were parading before the provost sergeant. The 'provo', nicknamed 'Cod's eyes', barked a few orders and dismissed us to our duties. From then on, for four days, I reported to the guardroom for half an hour's work before breakfast, again at 4.45pm for jobs or parades until 9.45pm. The jobs varied between cleaning a fireplace with hearthstone and washing pans or scrubbing tables in the mess hall. If there were no jobs they invented some, such as parading at your bed in best dress with all your kit laid out for inspection. CB meant 'confined to barracks', but we rarely went out, so that part of the punishment was meaningless. It was the daily slog of humdrum jobs that was the punishment.

We learned that the staff manning the barrack blocks were concerned with administration and discipline, and comprised NCOs doing tours of duty from the regular army: some from Infantry Regiments, others from Technical Corps. The staff members assigned with teaching the trades in the workshops were all from Technical Corps, including the Royal Engineers, the Royal Army Service Corps, and the Royal Army Ordnance Corps. And of course there were classroom studies under NCOs from the Army Education Corps.

We were suddenly aware that Easter was upon us, and we would be going home for a few days leave. I knew that I had grown a bit, but my uniform was still slightly large. Like everyone else I made sure that my gear was as smart as I could make it. We had to wear the white belt and puttees for the journey home. Trousers were worn with the parts below the knees wrapped under those puttees, and it was these parts that were turned up inside the uppers. They were pressed flat under our mattresses ('biscuits') between cardboard or plywood, or even better by a hot electric iron - if I could borrow one. Then the puttees took a lot of practice to wrap on neatly. I did the best I could, but I sometimes thought that my British army uniform was not attractive - especially when I stood behind an officer on parade, an officer whose Sam Browne belt and riding boots gleamed like glass, and whose superfine uniform was beautifully pressed. Such thoughts I kept to myself.

Came the day, and we trooped off to the station at Chepstow. We changed trains at the Severn Tunnel Junction, where civilians asked if we were cadets, and displayed little interest when we explained that we were apprentice tradesmen. By the time I had arrived at Bristol I was alone, and I travelled to my hometown of Camborne in the County of Cornwall without changing trains.

I walked up Camborne Hill, saw one or two people that I knew but didn't stop, and at my family farmhouse, named 'Tolcarne', I opened the back door and walked in, all choked up. They were all there: my father, mother, brother Kenneth, and sister Prudence. After embracing and kissing and staring, the talking started. Next day I saw a few boys I knew. Willy Truscott was an apprentice in a bicycle repair shop, learning very little I thought. Glen Eva was shovelling coal for Charlie Curnow the coal man, but he seemed quite happy. Some boys were luckier: they had been offered and accepted apprenticeships in Holmans where mining equipment was manufactured, and where they were taught fitting and machine operating and had several hours a week schooling. Glen had received such an offer, but couldn't afford to go. Apprentices got a mere two shillings and sixpence a week, so Glen chose to earn more shovelling coal, his mother being widowed. My few days were soon gone and I was on the train again.

Back at Beachley our trade studies continued. We practised wiring, using red and black covered wires, these being secured by ceramic cleats to wooden walls and ceilings. We became familiar with TRS (tough rubber sheathing), CRS (Cab Tyre Sheathing), VIR (Vulcanized India rubber) and other types of insulated cables, as well as screwed conduit that was sometimes used to house and protect cables.

At school we studied English, mathematics, and a subject called Army and Empire, under the AEC (Army Education Corps) instructors. We also had lessons in map reading, which was fascinating. Ordnance Survey maps were used, with a scale of one inch to one mile. We used army prismatic compasses, and learned the difference between true north and magnetic north. We examined a piece of contoured ground on the map, and then went out and walked over it.

At the end of a day, all of the apprentices attending the workshops paraded outside, and were called to attention by QMSI (Quartermaster Sergeant Instructor) Hanse, who then marched towards the officer commanding the parade, and barked out, "March off sir, pleeeeeze," with a vibrating salute where his fingers quivered like a tuning fork. The response was usually a very sleepy, "Carry on," whereupon each group marched up the hill to barracks. On most days we would naturally march to the workshops and back twice, and thought nothing of it. It was quite pleasant in fact along the barrack roads, the barracks being divided by grassed areas and regularly spaced mountain ash trees. On occasion we were paraded with our knives (cutlery knives) and spent an hour weeding the narrow beds that bordered the grass.

On one special day King George V's silver jubilee was celebrated, and we were served barley water and piccalilli relish with our cheese at teatime. We never saw these luxuries again - one wag (joker) reckoned that we would have to wait for the next king's silver jubilee. However, the few Methodists had a special treat once a month on a Friday evening. A parson used to come from Chepstow to hold RI (religious instruction), and after the prayers and a hymn he invariably produced a whole fruitcake to finish off. Most evenings were quiet, and I occasionally took out my watercolours and did a painting. A sergeant called Reid wandered in one evening and showed some interest, and finished up buying a watercolour of a full-rigged ship for one shilling and sixpence. He seemed pleased with the deal, and I certainly was.

As the weather got warmer, there were more outdoor activities. We became involved in all sorts of track and field events, and noticed a boy corporal called Sutherland from Poole who was a very determined middle distance runner. He didn't look an athlete, being quite thick around the waist, for which he was nicknamed 'Bread' (short for bread basket). He was about two years older than us, being in 33 Group, and used to win races by sheer determination. One day the school woke up to see a white flag flying from a two hundred foot electric pylon on the Welsh side of the Wye, and it bore the notice: 'Up 33 Gp'. Among the officers, NCOs and boys in the group all staring at it was the Commanding Officer, Colonel Shiels. The adjutant was heard to say, "The boy who did that will be caught and punished!" whereupon Colonel Shiels said, "No, there'll be no action taken." It was evident that the person who had put the flag there had crossed the Wye, with either its strong tide, or deep mud, or both, to pull off such a daring feat. Apparently no one knew the culprit, but most of us believed it was Bread. The 'flag' turned out to be an army sheet.

In November of that year we were informed that we would be representing the school in the Armistice parade at Chepstow, and on the 11th we duly set off in our best dress, with white belts, and boots and buttons gleaming. We arrived at the iron bridge and broke step, (as marching troops do when crossing a bridge) just as it started to rain. The war memorial was half way up the steep main street, and we were marched into our positions on four sides of a square surrounding the memorial, where four soldiers from the South Wales Borderers had taken up positions close to the corners. Throughout the proceedings, while a padre read prayers, the four soldiers held still in the position of 'Rest on your arms reversed', where the rifle is vertical and the muzzle is placed on the left boot, the arms being in an attitude of prayer over the butt of the rifle, and the head bowed. Two minutes of silence were observed, and a maroon (signal rocket) was fired. The rain pelted down. At the conclusion we marched the three miles or so back to the barrack blocks, with it still raining. An occasion to remember!

The boy corporal in charge of our room, a pale foxy-looking fellow with deep-set eyes, had been told that he would be going to the Corps of his choice, the Royal Army Service Corps, after the Christmas holiday, and woe betide anybody who said some other Corps was preferable. He obtained a set of RASC buttons and secured them to a piece of stiff cardboard. Any boy criticized for the slightest demeanour was 'punished' by having to clean those buttons. Ultimately a boy was instructed to sew those buttons onto a tunic - by tomorrow - but he had no thread, and the boys left in the room had none either. The corporal had gone off somewhere, but the boy decided he had to do something - so he used wool. The next day the corporal demanded to see the tunic - and exploded with rage. The boy protested he could do little else. The corporal announced that the boy was 'taking the Mickey' and would be dealt with by the wing sergeant. The wing sergeant did not appear, but Boy Sergeant Court did, and he listened with a straight face to the corporal's story and to the boy's story. Court asked lots of questions, to the point where the corporal appeared to be slowly losing his patience. The listening group of boys were straight faced too. The serious-faced group made off elsewhere and the affair fizzled out. When the corporal was seen wearing the tunic later, the buttons were on securely, sewn on no doubt by the corporal himself.

Shortly before the Christmas holiday a boy from our room reported sick with what proved to be measles, so we were put in isolation. We were not allowed to go anywhere near other boys, had limited exercise, and became bored stiff. One boy thought he could stand on a mantle shelf and jump for the nearest beam, about ten feet above the floor and eight feet away from him, and catch hold of it. He was successful so a couple more did it. Meantime two boys went to the cookhouse at the appointed time and brought back pans of hot food. The cheering that went on brought Corporal Jarvis from his room, and in his usual bossy way he stated that all boys were to do the jump before anyone fed. Pegg was now on the mantle shelf and hesitated a long time, trying to make up his mind. Finally he made an almighty jump, gripped the beam but continued swinging until he was horizontal, by which time his fingers had pulled off the top of the beam, and he fell ten feet down on to the hardwood floor. He writhed in agony, trying to get his breath, and fought off all attempts to help him. Jarvis was completely shocked, realizing that he would be held responsible. Pegg slowly recovered, the faces around him registering pity, surprise, fear, concern and relief. Relief especially when a white-faced Pegg finally said that he felt all right. He had got his wind back and just felt a bit sore. Jarvis said nothing and the rest of us sat down to eat. A few days later we all departed on leave, several days late.

At home my brother Kenneth was on leave from the RAF apprentices' college at Cranley. He was smart in his uniform: tunic breeches and puttees in air force blue. My sister had grown, and was quite beautiful. Her accent was very Cornish and my parents were doing what they could to help in her education, providing her with a piano on which she was making poor progress. She had made friends with Sylvia Retallack, who played the piano wonderfully, which seemed to help somewhat.

Shortly after our return for the first term in 1936, King George the Fifth died - on January 20th. This was much in the news because the heir to the throne, Edward, Prince of Wales, was determined to marry Mrs. Wallis Simpson, an American divorcee. Some thought that he would give up any thoughts of marrying Mrs. Simpson to become Edward VIII, while others thought that he would abdicate. The affair dragged on, with politicians and the Prime Minister involved, and the papers were full of it. One boy obtained a set of RASC buttons with the monogram of Edward VIII on them and was busily buffing and polishing them while waiting for his posting.

It was during this year that the school hospital became concerned over the number of boys with tonsillitis, and wrote to the parents of these boys seeking their approval for carrying out tonsillectomies. I was included, and duly went into hospital for the tonsil pulling with twenty or so others. I had been there before, and recalled a day when our doctor, Major Shields, was doing his rounds and came to a bed where the boy had prepared himself by pulling his pyjama trousers down and his jacket up. He thereby exposed his crotch where he had a large boil, and he watched the doctor's approach with interest in his face. Major Shields stared at him for a moment, then barked, "Move your balls, boy!" which he swiftly did while our diminutive matron stared at the floor pretending that she had not heard. We patients were trying hard to keep straight faces. At the next bed Major Shields ruled that the boy was not ready to leave hospital, no doubt because the patient's temperature was recorded as being high. This boy spent some time each day sitting on radiators and humming songs like "Dancing With My Shadow" and "Painting The Clouds With Sunshine" in order to keep his temperature up, because he liked it in hospital. I didn't like it there because the nursing sister soon found that I could make a good box crease when making up beds, so she grabbed me every day for that chore.

The sister, a member of QAIMNS (Queen Alexandra's Imperial Military Nursing Service), was quite a beauty, but with a reserved demeanour and completely encased in the stiff and starched uniform which they wore. On this occasion we were put to bed in two wards with a small treatment room in between. After 'lights out' we prowled around and quickly discovered that the medical operating tools were laid out in the small room. There were forceps of incredible shapes, mysterious tools for unknown purpose, and even a saw that was little different from a carpenter's tenon saw. I didn't sleep very well. Next morning we stayed in bed, the little room being screened off, and the first boy entered it, in his pyjamas.

Shortly afterward, the RAMC orderly came in and removed the boy's sheets, replacing them with a rubber ground sheet. A few minutes later the first boy was wheeled back into the ward on a stretcher. Then the orderly and a nursing sister lifted him onto the ground sheet and wiped a trickle of blood from his mouth. He was pale but looked okay. I was next, and I was glad, wanting to get it over. Inside, I climbed on to the table, with Matron and the sister making soothing noises, and Major Shields as the surgeon nearby. Matron placed a pad over my nose and told me to count. I think I counted to seven. Then I opened my eyes and I was on my ground sheet, feeling a bit faint. When I tried to swallow it felt terrible, as if a cricket ball was jammed there. Two boys nearby were staring at me with some concern, but I ignored them. I couldn't speak anyway. A few days later I felt fine.

It was about then that I remember marching back from workshops and seeing our band on a quiet road near the NAAFI doing a slow stride, and playing the Funeral March. A boy junior to us had died from meningitis, and was to be buried in the local Beachley churchyard. The whole company would attend. Instead of our school padre, the Beachley vicar, Captain Selwyn Cox, conducted the service. It was impressive. We had approached the church in that slow march, with the Funeral March being played. Then we paraded in the churchyard, Captain Kennedy and the commandant, Colonel Lawson, being present for the first part of the service. There were a number of civilians there, and we assumed they included the dead boy's relatives. The remainder of the service was held inside the church, which was not large enough for the whole company. One lady looked very tearful when the bugler played the Last Post. Finally, we marched back to barracks at quick time.

Our wing sergeant at that time, Sergeant Greaves of the Royal Tank Corps, was replaced by Sergeant Gallagher from the Highland Light Infantry, a unique battalion that wore trews (tartan trousers) instead of kilts. CSM Slee had gone too, and was replaced by CSM Dan Godfrey of the Border Regiment.

I was chatting with Bernard Hill one evening when we decided to look at the orchards along the road towards Sudbury, and we also decided to stuff our beds to make them appear occupied. I thought mine looked most realistic. The 'head' was almost covered, with just a wisp of hair showing from a concealed broom. Bernard did the same to his bed in another room. Off we went, taking cap comforters (a sort of knitted scarf) and choosing a little used route. We found an orchard, having walked nearly to Sudbury. We tried various trees and found some sweet apples. It was scary, hearing strange noises while being stuck high on a branch, filling our cap comforters, which we had cut open at one end. We were lucky. No dogs barked and we got away, trotting along the main road. The camp was in darkness, and we entered our respective barrack rooms. As I approached my bed Len Roots sat up in bed and said, "Harry, they're on to you," and a second later the lights came on as the door was kicked open by a military policeman who announced, "Dunstan, report to the Guard Room." This I did, and there I was warned that tomorrow I would be on a charge.

The next morning at the company office I was marched in by CSM Godfrey, alone, and the charge was read out. It was namely that I had been absent without leave from 2132 hrs to 0117 hrs ...blah...blah...blah. Meantime, Captain Kennedy's protruding eyes were boring into me. Then he demanded, "Where were you?"

"Out walking around, Sir."

"Why? Are you in trouble of some sort?"

"No Sir."

"Ten days CB. March him out, Sergeant Major."

Outside the sergeant major kept me standing to attention while he kept questioning me. Where did I go? How far did I go? Was I alone? Was I sure I was alone? Who did I meet? Then he told me to stand at ease, and he walked around me, putting on a stupid simpering look. He said everyone had problems, especially with girls, and it would be all right and would soon be cleared up. He said that I must not be afraid to ask for help, "Because we are here to help when you need help. Don't go off worrying about things late at night..."

I was getting very tired of this, his face so near mine, and the near smarmy innuendoes, so I blurted it out, "It was apples, Sir. I went out for apples." He stared at me, anger coming into his face. "Apples!" he cried, "Apples! Apples! Get to the guardroom! Double March!" His voice broke as he squeaked with rage, and I doubled off to begin my 'jankers', the army punishment and restriction of privileges issued for a relatively minor offence or breach of discipline.

Back in the barrack room that evening after my 'janker' chores, I listened to different boys' versions of what had happened. After Bernard Hill and I had left to go 'scrumping', Sergeant Gallagher had wandered in and started chatting, and had then noticed my mandolin lying on top of my locker. He had picked it up and stroked the strings, and said, "Do you play this thing? Hey, Dunstan, do you play this thing?" and then gave the shape in the bed a shove, dislodging the blanket and exposing the broom. Exploding, he stomped off to report the incident to the guardroom. Later he visited Hill's barrack room and started to tell them all what stupid fools they were in the next room (mine), thinking that they could pull the wool over his eyes - unaware that he was standing right next to Hill's stuffed bed.

Occasionally we would walk along the bank of the Wye to where it joined the Severn. At low tide we walked across the rocks and seaweed to St. Tecla's Isle, where there was a small lighthouse but little else, apart from the ruins of some ancient building. It was not a place to hang about because the tide came in very fast. I had once watched the water swirling there, shortly after the ebb had started. A gusty breeze was blowing from the west, but the water from the Severn was glassy, with whorls and dimples formed by deep eddies. The water from the Wye was choppy, the breeze taking tufts of spray from the wave tops. A flock of wild ducks came paddling from the east. They swept straight into the choppy water, bouncing up and down, appearing to enjoy it.

We sometimes walked further, to the jetties where the diesel-powered ferries were berthed. These vessels lowered a ramp to service the seven or eight cars that they carried on or off. They were called the Severn King and the Severn Queen, and it was a pleasure to watch the speed at which they manoeuvred when the tide was running fast. It used to make me shiver watching the muddy water, which almost always seemed to be covered with either spinning whirlpools or mighty upwellings. Only at high tide was the water placid for a short while before it started to ebb once again.

We rarely saw other craft on the water, except for the salmon boats. These came from Chepstow, and did their fishing far downstream on the Severn before returning. They were big heavy boats, controlled by one man with an oar over the stern. But he seemed to do very little except keep the craft where the current was strongest, because they only made the journey when the tide was favourable, and even then only when the salmon were running. We had heard of paddle steamers taking day-trippers from Bristol to Chepstow, but never saw any. I only ever watched one sizeable boat on the Severn, travelling downstream with the slow thump of its diesel sounding clearly across the sliding expanse of water. There were plenty of other boys, however, who had seen substantial boats on the Severn, plying between Scandinavia and Gloucester, supplying timber to the 'Blue Cross' match-making company.

One day we saw that a large circle of white canvas was spread out on the ground near the point, and were told that a round Britain air race was to take place. These planes appeared from the northeast, following the Severn. They were only fifty feet or so above the water, and on passing Beachley they altered course further to the south as they roared off downriver. Seeing only four of them, spaced well away from each other, we got bored and left.

Back in class we were now being lectured and tested and writing essays in three subjects - Math, English and Army & Empire. Only the first two were comparable to the subjects being taught in civilian schools. Our instructor was Sergeant Pawson, and during the year he finished his tour of duty and was replaced by Sergeant Owen. Both came from the Army Education Corps, and were university graduates. I found it interesting to hear their accents, especially when they were talking to boys with strong county accents. On one occasion during class we were each in turn asked to describe a personal happening, so when my turn came I stood up and recounted taking cattle through the woods to water, and nearly getting swept off the pony when passing through some close-knit saplings. This was well received, and I got a good applause that made my day. Listening to the other stories made me realize how fortunate I had been to spend my early years on a farm in the country. In our studies we were aiming to pass exams leading to the award of army certificates of education. We found the second-class exam quite easy. For the first-class exam we would find that some serious study was necessary.

When the weather was good there was plenty of work to be done on a power line project. The existing lines were being replaced with a 'ring main', which would provide the means of isolating small sections for repair while continuing to supply power to the main area. We did everything, from digging holes for individual poles to running the cables from pole to pole. A couple of us were watching Raynor, who was almost out of sight digging in the bottom of a hole, when Colonel Shiels appeared with the usual entourage, and peered down the hole while making some profound comments. Blissfully unaware, Raynor switched from pick to shovel and heaved up a load of wet mud, which he dumped on the CO's gleaming boot! There was the noise of indrawn breath all round as Raynor looked up, his expression registering shock as he quickly mumbled, "Very sorry Sir..."

"Oooh...ah...it's quite all right," said the CO and moved off quickly, making more profound comments. We found it amusing that on one of the rare moments when such a god-like personage as the CO should visit us, we piled wet mud on him.

Generally we found outdoor work very enjoyable after spending time in class, even in cold weather. When stringing cables, we had to shut off the power for a short time while isolating a section. And once Sergeant Chandler came himself with a helper and a bucket of tea to encourage the speedy return of power. In the barracks, the wiring had to be replaced in some rooms, usually using twin or three-core cable secured with bend-over clips. On one job, I was running a long piece of cable and found that it was too short to enter the brass connector by about an inch. I then did a bad thing, which was to have, for me, far reaching consequences. I added a piece of cable, twisting the wires together and covering the joint with a scrap of insulating material. I then put the cover on the joint and it looked fine.

Days later I was up among the beams lying on my back on a plank when I became aware that Corporal Griffiths was demanding, "Who was he? The sneak! Who was the sneak who did this? Which one of you is it?"

"It was me, Corporal. I did it," I said hastily as I scrambled down.

And then followed a long berating while I was stripping down the cable and replacing it. I was glad when the day was over, and thought that was the end of the matter. But next day I was sent for by Mechanist Sergeant Major Easterbrook, one of the older staff who dressed in superfine khaki with a plain hooked-up collar. He addressed me seriously but not unkindly, and quoted from the IEE Regs (Institute of Electrical Engineers Regulations) explaining how such joints were to be made. He made it clear that I must do better, and then dismissed me. A few days later I was warned for interview with Lieutenant Seagrim, the company second-in-command. I had been placed on the 'black list'. A week later I was told to report to the administration block in best dress for interview with the Commanding Officer. I duly appeared, with boots and buttons gleaming, but feeling very low. Inside, the Regimental Sergeant Major inspected me. Then I waited for what seemed an age. Finally I was marched in to the CO's office. I was very tense, wondering what was coming, but he surprised me. He talked quietly about my work, mentioned some reports. Then he advised me to work hard, and I was marched out. In six months I was off the 'black list'.

I was not conscious of any special educational effort, just of trying to understand the various ideas and theories we were being taught. I knew that I was learning some things 'parrot fashion', but that was because electricity was (and is) to me something unreal. You could pass a current through something, say a wire, and afterwards observe no evidence of its passing, apart from perhaps some heating effect. Then, when I learned for example Fleming's right hand rule, I understood that if you did certain things then other specific things would result, and one could calculate the outcome precisely. So anyway, I suppose that I was a slow learner.

It was during this year that a new wing sergeant, called Upton, appeared. He was a big heavy man, over six feet, and quite pleasant under a severe exterior, so we called him 'Tiny'. He was a good drill instructor, and taught us to march with precision, to listen to the feet hitting the ground and to ensure that your feet were precisely in with the others. It worked well. With him we drilled on asphalt, never on gravel, and the sound certainly was clear-cut. Things were not so pleasant in our visits to the gymnasium. The sergeants who took charge there were from the APTS (Army Physical Training Staff) and a new one was more than enthusiastic. He kept us leaping, jumping, stretching and running till we staggered around, whacked out. There being no let up or encouragement, we sulked, and deliberately slowed our movements, failing even to start immediately following an order. He reacted predictably by getting even more abusive. We moaned whenever there was the slightest reason, but not so that he could hear us clearly, so he couldn't charge us. Soon the APTS sergeant major, called Dennison, noticed the tension and appeared in person during a training session in place of the sergeant. He talked to us quietly and said that if the situation worsened, as appeared likely, we would be the losers.

"After all," he said, "Who are you working for?" pausing to stare at us with a serious expression.

"Ourselves," several boys said.

He said nothing further, just quietly looked at us, and then dismissed us. At the next session we worked hard, and the sergeant had certainly cooled off. Soon the whole thing appeared to be forgotten, but we watched that sergeant closely for a long time.

We received instruction in boxing techniques - footwork and balance - using the gloves in attack and defence, and all sorts of things that did not interest me in the slightest. How anyone could consider it a sport when two people hammered the daylights out of each other completely escaped me. We had annual elimination bouts where everyone fought at least once. Last year (1935) I had been matched against Ginger Greenwood, a blacksmith who had no trouble in duffing me around the ring. This year I was matched against Jimmy Neeve, so I approached him with a suggestion that we should both take it easy, and I was prepared to pay him two shillings! Jimmy laughed it off and said that he had been thinking of approaching me with a similar proposal. On the evening that we fought he had no trouble in keeping me off with a straight left arm, while he belted me quite hard at times with his right hand, smiling kindly all the while.

The night of the 1936 finals was quite an occasion as various trophies were presented with due ceremony. After the finals were finished, a boxing team invited from Malvern College visited us. They came, with their supporters, and on arrival were given a rousing cheer by us all. The bouts were held in the gymnasium, which was packed; everyone sitting on benches or ranged along the walls. As usual there was no referee in the ring, but there were two sitting at a table just outside it. On this occasion they were retired officers. When a referee wished to admonish a contender he called sharply, "Stop!" Then he said his piece and called out, "Box on!" Although our visitors fought well, and we supported them at every opportunity with loud cheers, they lost every bout. This was expected by many, considering that our team was the best from about eight hundred very fit boy soldiers. I was very happy that there were no serious injuries.

During this year at the workshops we studied 'Car Electrical', which I found fascinating, from the battery, the lead/acid cell which held stored electricity, and with which one could start a car, to all the mass of devices that enabled the internal combustion engine to operate. Whether providing light to shine on the road ahead or to illuminate the dashboard, the subject was packed with interest. This was complimented with 'Car

Mechanical', a course held in the machinery engineering workshops, where the mysteries of gearboxes, clutches and brakes were revealed.

In the school classroom we had completed our studies for the second-class certificate, passed our exams and were now studying for the first-class certificate. Among other things, this entailed studying a classical story, which for us was "Henry Esmond" by William Makepeace Thackeray. Try as I might to discover why this book was interesting, I always drew a complete blank. It was a story, yes, but what a boring one! I found that I had to memorise various sections of the story parrot-fashion, because any discussion about the book was completely devoid of interest.

During the time I was at school in Beachley I knew of only one case where a boy was charged with an offence involving an unacceptable sexual act, and that was a serious one, just before the Easter leave. A boy complained that a senior had sexually assaulted him; that he had in fact raped him. The accused was held in the guardroom during the leave, and then faced a court martial. None of this was made public, and the whole school was agog with rumours and hearsay. We were not aware what a court martial entailed in the regular army, much less for boy soldiers. In the event, a civilian solicitor appeared for the defence and another for the prosecution, and both the plaintiff and the defendant were cross-examined. In the end the defendant was sentenced to be discharged with ignominy. It was said that many boys who knew those who were involved believed that the plaintiff was not blameless, being "an effeminate pansy with an unnatural liking for other boys", and that he had likely encouraged the encounter.

Shortly afterwards a general, no less, visited the school and addressed us, a small group at a time. He was livid and could hardly contain himself, and I couldn't understand a word he said except for 'disgraceful' and 'shameful behaviour' sandwiched between lots of wuff-wuff noises coming out from his thick white moustache. He then departed, still fuming. Those to whom the plaintiff had reported were a boy sergeant, who had his stripes taken away, and the regular wing sergeant, who was replaced.

Besides 'Pesky' Milliner, there was another civilian instructor called Potter, nicknamed 'Gillie' (after the English comedian and broadcaster Gillie Potter) who was very likeable. He always mixed in interesting topics that were additional to lectures on electricity, such as the rhyme illustrating the use of navigation lights at night. "Green to green and red to red - perfect safety, go ahead." There was also a Corporal Slade. He was serious, friendly and always ready to discuss any problem arising from lectures. I remember him discussing gravity and its effect on the tides, how the pull of the sun together with that of the moon combined to produce spring tides, which had such massive effects on the water levels of the rivers around us.

Sergeant Russell on the other hand was very different, being a showman given the slightest opportunity. He once recited Gunga Din in the classroom, with one eye on the corridor outside in case someone approached. Another time he demonstrated, behind his back, how to splice a loop in the centre of a length of rope without cutting it, a very entertaining party trick, which of course had nothing to do with electricity. On one occasion, knowing that a senior officer would be visiting us, he first practised delivering a couple of paragraphs on the subject of providing high voltage at precisely timed intervals for an internal combustion engine, then pretended to study some notes while standing near the door and carefully watching the approach corridor. We heard Major Tickell coming with the senior visitor and various others, whereupon Sergeant Russell started to repeat the paragraphs he had previously rehearsed in a loud and grandiose manner. He stopped immediately the door opened and gave the visitor a superb salute, and then explained what the lecture was about in a strange theatrical voice that we had not heard before, but nevertheless found very entertaining. Such occasions were the exception rather than the rule. Most workshop classes entailed a steady slog at learning, which involved wading through the mysteries of joules, farads, ohms and watts, followed by writing everything in longhand.

1936 drew to a close with the news that Edward (nearly the Eighth) had abdicated on 11th December, and that his brother, the Duke of York, was to be King George VI. I suppose we felt a bit cynical about the whole thing. We, of course, were sworn to serve the King, his heirs and successors, et cetera, but we knew very well that we did not in any practical sense take any command from the king. He was just there, occupying a traditional monarchy position, a figurehead. We were more concerned with the daily duties that we faced.

From time to time we were given instruction on additional forms of drill. The drill system was based, to a large extent, on the need to move a body of men, which we will call a squad, in a column four abreast. It could easily be changed to two abreast, or to an extended line that was only two deep, or even to single file. After forming into two lines, the command, "Number," was given. The right hand man in the front rank called, "One," and the man next to him called, "Two," and so on until all the men in the front rank were numbered. Those who were in the rear rank noted the numbers called, each man assuming the number of the man in front of himself. If it was then decided to move this body of men to the right as a column four abreast, the order given was, "Move to the right in fours... form fours," upon which all even numbers moved so that they were standing behind the man on their right. That is, each man moved one pace to the rear with his left leg, then one pace to the right with his right leg, finally bringing his left leg close to his right leg. Then came the order, "Right," and the whole squad turned right and were ready to march off. This was the essential basis of 'fours' drill, and having practised this, we progressed to other more complicated drill movements.

The Final Year At Beachley

In the following year - 1937 - being seventeen years old, we had now become the seniors. Ginger Fordham had been made Boy Regimental Sergeant

Major; Cockle became Company Sergeant Major; Ray Ballard and George Garwood became Boy Sergeants. The rest of us in 35 Group never addressed them by their rank; only juniors did that. Not that this meant any disrespect - that's just how it was.

In the electrical trade training we were dealing with ever more difficult calculations, and on the practical side, among other duties, we provided electrical power for a block of brand new classrooms. We also attended short courses on other trades. The reasoning behind this was that wherever electrical work was required the electricians would often find it necessary to disturb paintwork, wood or concrete flooring, masonry walls or steelwork. So an electrician had to be able to make good any disruption he caused and to leave a place as good as he found it. In the painters' shop we learned how to grind and mix pigments and to use oils, dryers and thinners. We cut stencils and applied them for various purposes. We built block walls in the masons' shop, and then built more walls with bricks. We learned how to make a timber former for a brick arch, add the arch and remove the former the next day. Then back to electricity, where we stripped a burned out motor and rewound the field coils and armature windings, using wooden formers that we had made for the job. Next a turning lesson using small Drummond lathes, and this job included turning the armature for which we had made new segments during our repair of the motor.

For Easter I had accepted an invitation to spend the leave with Len Roots, and so with his younger brother, Victor, we made our way to Corsham via Bristol. My sister, Prudence, was studying to be a Nursery Nurse at Downend College, and she was at Bristol Temple Meads station to see us. I was proud of her - she was quite beautiful - and I was amused to see how shy and tongue-tied Len had become. After a meal with her we pressed on to Corsham. The leave was memorable because the Roots' hospitality was superb. Len's father, a stolid, heavy police inspector, had duties at the Box Tunnel installation, a maze of tunnels linked to the Great Western Railway tunnel, which we visited. Len's mother was slim and vivacious, and had organized a number of parties where we drank a fair quantity of beer and sang a lot. We also went to the Windmill Theatre in London where many old men occupied the front seats ensuring a good view of the posed nudes appearing in some routines. Such exposures were permitted providing the nudes kept perfectly still. Then back to Corsham and more parties, and more experimenting with alcoholic drinks, with pipes and with cigarettes, all of which tended to make us sick, and which we normally did without at Chepstow. Then the journey back to Chepstow, memorable because as we were pulling out of Corsham station Len drew my attention to a small figure waiting for the London train - it was the Emperor Haile Selassie of Abyssinia who had sought asylum in England after Italy had invaded his country.

We had not been back at Chepstow for long when the coronation of King George VI took place, and some time later the whole school went to Newport to form a guard of honour for the king's visit. For us this entailed lining both sides of the roads and streets along the route leading from the railway station. We were five feet apart with the crowd behind us, with a policeman every hundred feet. We assumed that the policeman was there for crowd control. Behind me were several girls, one who kept digging me in the back and making remarks like, "Who d'you think you are? A film star or a cowboy or something?" to the accompaniment of squawks and giggles. I stared straight ahead and didn't move a muscle. After a while the vehicle appeared with King George VI and Queen Elizabeth (the mother of Queen Elizabeth II, later known as the Queen Mother). They passed by slowly in the limousine, waving languidly. The Queen was on the left side of the car, my side, so I enjoyed my first good look at a queen. I thought she was rather plump with a pleasant expression as her eyes ranged over the crowd, her left hand meanwhile waving slowly up and down almost as if she was painting a fence in slow motion. King George on the far side simply raised his forearm from the elbow and was revolving his open hand in a small circle. The din was terrific; plenty of 'oohs' and 'aahs', and small flags waving, and a band nearby with a very keen bass drummer making a lot of noise.

Afterwards we marched to a recreation ground where we were given some food, and then our gymnastics team put on a demonstration that they had been working on for weeks. The highlight was when the team split into two lines that passed through each other at right angles and at speed, with hand stands, back flips, vaults and somersaults, earning themselves some hearty cheers and prolonged clapping from the crowd. Then we wandered around the town and met some girls who were quite happy to go to the cinema with us, where we became involved in some gentle wrestling in the seats. Quite a pleasant day.

As a Methodist, I often thought it was a bit strange the way we had to attend church. On Sundays the comparatively few Methodists attended a separate parade from the Church of England procedure. But on weekdays the whole school attended the short morning service taken by the padre, the Reverend Selwyn Cox. A collection was made daily, but I never knew any boy who put anything in it. The Rev. Cox used to get very cross about that. He had plans for any money collected. One day he announced that he was arranging for a small sum to be stopped from each boy's pay, whereupon the commandant stood up in the front row and said, "That will not take place!" and sat down. Considering that even senior boys only drew a few shillings per week, we understood the commandant's action perfectly.

As the year drew to a close, we were all thinking of the new life that the next year would bring. I had chosen to go to the RE's (Royal Engineers) along with two thirds of the electricians and all four of the instrument mechanics. Among them were George Garwood, Ray Ballard, Ginger Fordham and Len Roots. And also Roy Shearman, although he was later to transfer to the RAOC (Royal Army Ordnance Corps), as he had originally intended. So the electricians who went to the RAOC were ultimately six, and they were all later drafted to Palestine. Only one, 'Wocko' Watkinson, went to the Royal Tank Corps; Bolton went to the RASC (Royal Army Service Corps).

Chatham

After our Christmas leave, we returned and were soon posted to our new units. Those of us joining the RE's arrived at Chatham railway station, loaded our kit bags into a truck, and then paraded for the march to a small place four miles away called Chattenden. We marched through Chatham led by the RE Fife & Drum band, an unexpected surprise. I felt self-conscious marching behind a thumping big drum and the squeaky flutes and piccolos, but they soon left us. On arrival we found Chattenden to be a small barracks and ourselves the only occupants. Two corporals called Steer and Parmenter were in charge of us, living in our barrack rooms. They were fine chaps, cheerful and, of course, strict when necessary. Parmenter was known as 'Yank' but actually he was a Canadian. We soon settled in, and were issued with the full webbing equipment: large pack, haversack, five-a-side pouches, water bottle, a rifle, a bayonet and a 'tin hat'. World War One gear in fact. We started square-bashing with a vengeance, including drill with rifle and bayonet.

"Squad will fix bayonets...FIX!" whereupon the rifle was pushed forward (from the 'order arms' position) while the left hand grabbed the bayonet handle and half withdrew it with the arm vertically against the body.

"BAYONETS!" at which time each man's left arm jerked forward and engaged the bayonet, his arm remaining there while he listened for the right hand man's signal.

The right hand man, having satisfied himself that all were ready, squawked out, "RIGHT!" whereupon each man pulled his rifle back to the 'order arms' position.

This was usually followed by, "SLOPE ARMS." On the second occasion we did this, one man's bayonet flew off and penetrated the sleeve of the man in the rear rank. The sergeant drilling us maintained a straight face, in fact a plummy bored expression, while the culprit recovered his bayonet from the man behind him, replaced it on his rifle and sloped arms.

We learned to dig a trench in the style that was developed on the Western Front, complete with 'A' frames, duckboards and a fire step. Following the order, "Prepare to go over," you mounted the fire step, with your left forearm on the berm and also supporting your rifle muzzle. Your right hand gripped the rifle near the small of the butt, and your eyes covered the ground ahead, with your 'tin hat' just clear of the parapet. A thought swept through my mind the first time I had to do it. This was what British soldiers were doing in France a generation ago! They were dressed the same way too: 'tin hat', five-a-side ammunition pouches, water bottle and the rest.

Knots-and-lashings was a popular subject, and we used poles and cordage (ropes) to construct derricks, gins and shear-legs (lifting devices using one, two or three poles) and used them to move heavy weights about. We were very soon made aware that as men in the Royal Engineers we were soldiers first, then sappers (combat engineers) and then tradesmen. So in this phase of sapper training we were going to learn pontoon bridge building, and as a prelude to this we learned to row. We did this first using eight and ten-oared gigs - heavy clinker built boats on which the poppets along the sides were removed to allow the heavy ash wood oars to be located for rowing. This was done in the nearby Medway where the tides ran fast and we rowers had to allow for them. (We also discovered that Corporal Parmenter kept a kayak somewhere nearby, and often explored the river.)

Rowing was most enjoyable work. A crew would file on board and take their places. First there was a bow-man who would use the boat hook when laying alongside another craft or a jetty. Then the rowers, sitting in pairs and facing the stern, and finally the cox (or coxswain) who would sit in the stern and command the crew. Any passengers would also sit in the stern. On the command, "Oars!" each rower took an oar and raised it to a vertical position with the blade 'feathered' into the wind or with the blade aligned fore and aft if there was no wind. He would also remove the poppet in the side of the gig, leaving a slot that would later accommodate the oar. The cox would then instruct the bow-man to "shove off," or take what other steps were necessary to gain sea room. When the cox commanded, "Down oars," each rower let his oar fall outwards till it hit the water, then quickly put the loom of his oar into the slot and brought the oar to the horizontal with the blade parallel to the water. When a crew was practised, this was a pleasure to watch. The rowers would take their cue from the lead portside rower -

the 'stroke' as it was called - ensuring that all oars fell together and hit the water with a resounding smack, and then assume the horizontal together. The usual succeeding orders were, "Stand by to give way," and then, "Give way... all!"

There were many other orders to be followed to ensure safe manoeuvring of the boat. After much practise at rowing and general watermanship we paraded one day in full marching order, boarded the gigs on the River Medway and rowed the four miles or more to a Royal Naval jetty near the Royal Engineer barracks in Chatham. We disembarked, assembled smartly, and marched through the naval yards, past the RE workshops, and up to the memorial arch opposite the SME (School of Military Engineering). Then past the bronze statue of General Gordon on his camel, and on to the main parade ground of the training battalion fronting Brompton Barracks. Here we carried out various drill manoeuvres under the watchful eye of QM Sergeant 'Kim' Hargreaves, the Senior Drill Instructor of the battalion, who walked with a fierce swagger and sported a Sam Browne belt (and was best avoided whenever possible). General Bond, the 'Officer Commanding', then inspected us. When he came to me, he stood quite still and gazed into my face for a few seconds. I subsequently realized that he was doing this to each man, more or less, as if committing each face to memory. After the inspection, we went marching back to the naval jetty, and then to Chattenden by rowing. An unusual day.

We received instruction in rifle shooting at a range east of Gravesend and near the Thames.

Accommodation was in Shornmead Fort, the old gun emplacements now converted to small barrack rooms. We marched there from Chattenden, our kitbags going by truck. The countryside was absolutely flat, wet in places, and deserted apart from us. Every day we marched to the range where the red flag was flown to warn anyone approaching that firing was in progress. For most of the time I was in the group being coached by Corporal Steer, and I remember those times with pleasure. I learned to form a tripod with my chest and two elbows, pulling the rifle close in to my shoulder to squeeze the trigger slowly while momentarily holding my breath. We took our turn in the rifle butts where we signalled to the would-be marksmen to advise them where their shots had fallen. Afterwards, we would queue up to 'boil out', each waiting his turn to use the funnel to pour boiling water through his rifle barrel. When not on the range we could roam the banks of the Thames, follow the riverside footpath into Gravesend past the hulk that housed young Royal Navy sailors, and then at the end march back to Chattenden.

Life at Chattenden was very different from Beachley, and I for one rarely thought about Beachley. There were some old pals, and some new from the other Chepstow companies that I hardly knew before: O'Donnell, Peck, Walker, Kerr and others. There were new rules, new surroundings. The countryside was worth exploring, and on one long walk three of us, Roots, Garwood and I, discovered a dewpond. It had to be a dewpond because it was on the crest of a rounded hilltop, and it was ten feet deep and fringed with small trees. It was a very mild February day, with a brilliant sun, so we stripped naked and jumped in - for about fifteen seconds! Then we rubbed ourselves down with our underpants, dressed and walked back feeling wonderful, each with a pocketful of wet underpants. We could walk to the nearest pub, or to Chatham, every night if we wished. Twice, when I had walked to Chatham with a pal, we crossed the bridge over the Medway and saw a twin-engine flying boat sitting on the water near Short's workshops. Each time the flying boat was tethered in three directions with ropes that appeared surprisingly thin, and the craft moved gently, responsive to the slightest wave. The ropes dipped into the water and then emerged dripping, as we leaned on the parapet, reluctant to move on. I was never lucky enough to see a flying boat arrive or take off.

We could drink or smoke - not that I smoked, and I couldn't really afford to drink. Although I was in a man's army I was on boy's pay, because my 18th birthday was not until 14th June. There were several others 'in the same boat'. As ex-boy soldiers we were given somewhat different training to raw recruits joining straight from 'Civvy Street'. We completed our square-bashing with an involved passing-out parade at Brompton Barracks, and then dispersed. Some were posted to their final units, but we, the electricians, were housed in Kitchener Barracks while we undertook extra trade training. This was because the trade had to be more specifically suited to the needs of the Corps.

Included in this course was more ICE tuition (internal combustion engines). One machine, a

Tangye semi-diesel, had a huge flywheel, half of which was housed below floor level, and which had to be turned by hand ready for starting, a job requiring much grunting effort from a half-dozen men. Then the attached compressor was started and its air storage brought to the required pressure (if it wasn't there already) coincident with heating a chamber attached to the cylinder head with a blowlamp. To start up, air was admitted to the cylinder, and the flywheel started to turn. The automatically injected diesel oil was initially only partially vaporised and was ignited by the red-hot chamber, but, as the engine picked up speed, ignition also became automatic, and as the hot chamber cooled it was manually isolated. This giant machine rapidly attained its working speed and the spinning ten-foot wheel was most impressive, making hardly more than a whisper of noise as it puffed with each revolution. Normally the air storage was left at high pressure, so to start the machine only the correct positioning of the flywheel and heating the chamber were then required.

We also learned to use the searchlight located in the top floor of the SME. This involved starting the direct current generator and then bringing the electric arc carbons closer together until an electric spark jumped across the gap between them. The carbons were viewed through a small window of darkened glass. This white-hot arc was located in the metal cylindrical body of the searchlight, of about 5-foot diameter, and the resulting light rays were emitted in all directions, but only those which reached the back of the cylinder, about a quarter of the rays, were reflected by a parabolic dish to form the beam of light that one sees penetrating the night sky. This had us scratching our heads while thinking, "Why doesn't someone invent a system where *all* the light rays are reflected into a beam?" But we found that to be easier said than done.

A number of other subjects were studied before we were ready for our exams, and then we were posted to our various field units. We were advised that we would be recalled for an advanced electrician's course in September, giving us all some cause for satisfaction. We then went our various ways, and I, together with Ray Ballard and a most likable chap called Hall, who was a fitter, went to the 1st Field Squadron. O'Donnell and Walker, both carpenters, and Bernard Hill went to the 26th Field Company. These units were in Stanhope Lines, Gibraltar Barracks, Aldershot.

Aldershot

I was still a boy soldier, but I carried out the same duties as other sappers (combat engineers). We soon discovered that a Field Squadron was different from a Field Company. While a field company usually worked with an infantry division, a field squadron was part of a cavalry division, (now almost 100% mechanized) for whom it provided engineering duties. Our officers still retained a few horses, called officers' chargers. Instead of trousers and puttees we wore breeches and puttees, and also spurs. Although we had bayonets we usually paraded without them, and instead wore a brown belt and a leather 5-pouch bandolier slung from the left shoulder to under the right arm. We were distinctive, so we swaggered a bit. Although we shared the same guardroom as the field companies, and the same cookhouse and mess room, and the same NAAFI, we were different. Majors commanded field companies, but we were commanded by a lieutenant colonel. I guessed that this was because the several field companies were headed by majors who reported to a lieutenant colonel, but there was only one field squadron.

Our work involved bridge building, and we soon started working with a small box girder bridge. Sixteen-foot long box girders could be linked together to form, say, a sixty-four foot length, and laid across a river or gully to rest on prepared bankseats. More lengths could then be laid beside the first, and the whole structure could then be 'floored' using heavy planks that were held down securely by bolted ribbands. The carrying capacity of such bridges depended on the total distance bridged and the number of lengths placed side by side. The sixteen-foot girders were the heaviest items, and could be carried by eight men using a carrying pole for each pair of men. In the annual Tidworth Tattoo, a team from the Royal Engineers would demonstrate how this bridge was used, starting with the equipment laid out nearby. They would build a bridge across a 48-foot gully and send a tank across - all in a time of fifteen minutes.

Our commander was an inventive officer, and we were soon involved in trying out his ideas. One day we were experimenting with a mobile crane, to see if it could be used to push sections of small box girders across a gully. A cable from the boom to the end of the section was used to hold it horizontal. On another day we would be stringing steel cables across a canal (the nearby Basingstoke Canal) until there were enough to support planking for a road. Ordnance pattern holdfasts were employed, each being a 30-inch piece of steel with eight 24-inch steel pins driven through holes in it and into the bank. To stop the 'road' twisting like a ribbon, diagonal ropes were stretched under the roadway, and secured from bank to bank. Held in this way the 'bridge' would take a car, but when a 30-cwt truck attempted to cross, the contraption always started to twist. The driver kept easing his machine forward, trying slightly different parts of the road, but to no avail.

One idea was quite intriguing. The largest sized bridging truck arrived with a huge roll of canvas and stopped at the edge of a stretch of water, where we off-loaded it. When we rolled the canvas out flat with one end at the water's edge, we found that the end had to be supported by lengths of canvas bolster rolled into the canvas edge, while about 12 inches of the long sides were bent up and secured using little bamboo struts. We now had a big rectangle of canvas that, being stiffened by lengths of bamboo stitched into transverse seams, and with the canvas itself being waxed, was in effect a raft. To test it, we sappers eased it into the water and found that a number of us could easily walk about on it. Our weight bent the bamboo-stiffened canvas into the water, but the edges remained at water level.

Next, one end of the raft was positioned on the bank and the bolsters at that end removed. The truck was then driven slowly on to the raft and the bolsters replaced. The idea was a great success. The bamboo reinforced canvas bent to take the weight of the truck, but the edges of the canvas remained at water level. We sappers, tickled with the astounding result of the test, gave an enthusiastic cheer. We never heard whether such a method was ever developed further, but it stuck in our memories because a whole fleet of trucks could use one roll of canvas for a water crossing.

We were very fortunate in that we had a commanding officer who believed that his men should be trained in as many ways as possible. The 'Boys Anti-tank Rifle' (nicknamed the elephant gun because of its size and large bore) fired a half-inch diameter bullet, and was included in our training. The muzzle of this rifle had a disc of steel fitted in front of it and, behind that, the muzzle was slightly bell-mouthed. When it was fired, the bullet passed through the disc, and the exploding gas that followed it fanned out and struck the disc, thereby slightly lessening the effect of the recoil, but it was still a shattering weapon to fire. Unlike firing a Lee Enfield, one had to lie directly in line with the Boys rifle, which was rested on a bipod. My shoulder felt quite sore after firing it, which was understandable. The bore, and therefore the thrust, was 2.7 times that of a Lee Enfield rifle. This anti-tank rifle however was soon considered obsolete because of heavier armour being produced on the newer tanks. It was phased out in favour of the PIAT anti-tank gun that was developed in 1942 and used in WW2 from 1943 on.

We also learned to use a revolver, and a light field gun. And we were given driving instruction in every vehicle that was available to us, including a Norton motor cycle, a Hillman staff car, various infantry pick-up trucks, 30-cwt trucks, and the largest 10-wheel bridging truck with it's 4-wheel trailer. I had an amusing experience with the latter. Driving through Aldershot on market day I was negotiating a crossroads right in the middle of the town, and to ensure that my trailer didn't collide with a building, I had to mount the corner sidewalks with my front wheels - when I stalled the engine! To make it much worse, I couldn't find the starter button. Finally I remembered - it was under the seat. A friendly policeman was very helpful when he saw that some pedestrians were getting a little annoyed.

Learning to drive these different vehicles was challenging, but not always pleasant, especially in bad weather. The infantry pick-up trucks had small windscreens, with manually operated wipers. All trucks had a canvas-covered cab, and the big bridging trucks had a canvas dodger over which the driver had to peer - not pleasant in driving rain. The pick-up trucks also had a glass cylinder mounted on the dashboard that provided gravity fed fuel to the carburettor. It was kept full by a suction line from the inlet manifold on the engine, enabling it to draw fuel from the petrol tank. When completely full, a valve automatically closed the suction line.

In the middle of all this activity and training I celebrated my eighteenth birthday. I didn't feel any different, and after the birthday my military activities continued as before. My pay was increased: from 1 shilling and 5 pence per day as an apprentice to 3 shillings and 9 pence per day as a qualified electrician in the regular army, with effect from 14th June 1938.

So ended my three and a half years as a boy soldier, and I was now engaged to serve for eight years in man service, followed by four years in the army reserve, when I would be liable for call up. The thought that we might actually be involved in a war did not trouble me overmuch, or my colleagues. And I looked forward to the electrical course that would take place in September.

Corbie in northeast France

62

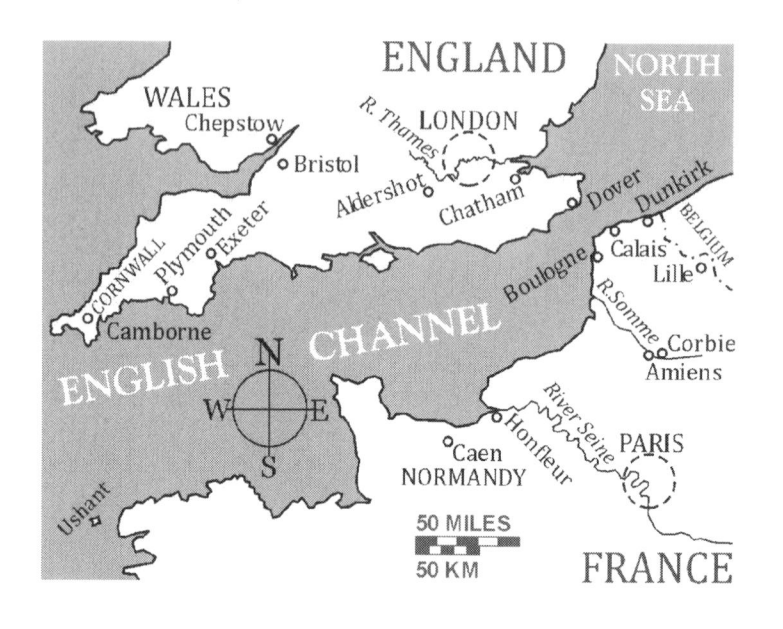

The Phoney War & Dunkirk
Chapter 1

I couldn't believe it really. I was here at the School of Military Engineering in Chatham, about to start a course for quite promising (were we?) students, when it was only Whitsunday last year that I was walking towards Paris, feeling rather fed up with the army and thinking quite seriously of trying something else - yes, that was it - deserting! I had not thought about it very carefully, and after three days in France I had decided to give myself up to a gendarme in the Rue de Montmartre. To cut a long story short, I was charged with being absent without leave (not desertion) and being in a foreign country without permission - so three days in the clink. But that was yesterday! Today I was here, and thinking that I was going to enjoy this.

There were seven or eight men that I knew from last year and from boy service: George Garwood, Ginger Fordham, Roy Shearman, Ray Ballard, Pete Moyser, and Hampton (Ammo). We were on the first floor of the school, having clattered up the stairs only minutes ago. The instructor had said he would be back, so we chatted, looking down from the windows and seeing men passing by, some of whom we knew. There was one, a sergeant, whom I remembered quite well from a year ago, although I had only seen him once. He had been taking us on a rare drill period, and had told the senior sapper in attendance to take over. The sapper had no expertise at all, and was very embarrassed, much to our entertainment, but my amusement rapidly disappeared when the sergeant selected me to replace him. My effort was hardly commendable, but the sergeant, seeing I was seriously trying, gave me some helpful instruction in calling parade ground orders. And so there he was, the second time I had ever seen him.

I was trying to remember his name when the instructor returned and made his announcement. The course was cancelled, and we were to report for military duties. War had been declared, and this cancellation was similar to that of last year. The interruption back then was the Munich Crisis, and on that occasion we had each just been issued with a set of instruments and other gear, when suddenly the class was disbanded, and instead of a lesson we were busy sandbagging buildings and rigging emergency lights. Then we were converting the underground tunnels near the school to makeshift accommodation. After a few days the scare blew over and we returned to our units.

This time it was different. Suddenly, Brompton Barracks, where we were housed, was on a wartime footing, as were the other RE barracks nearby, along with the marine and naval barracks. There were accounts of enemy aircraft over the town, and there was the noise of ack-ack and damage to roofs. The men manning the Lewis gun on the top of the memorial arch reported engaging the enemy at two thousand feet! We soon realized that the planes were our own, and that no one had recognized their markings on such a dull day. Fortunately, no pilot reported any damage. The roof damage due to anti-aircraft shrapnel was minimal. Within a day or so I was on my way to join the RE detachment of the 1st Bridge Company RASC, which was mustering somewhere near Aldershot, and me not knowing where my recent classmates were bound. When I arrived, I found that the detachment was about thirty-five strong, nearly all reservists, many of them wearing the ribbons of their WWI medals. They were led by a busy little man called Sergeant Gray, nicknamed 'Dolly Gray'. There was Gadd, a regular about my age, and among the reservists, Metcalfe, who was around thirty-two. Many seemed pretty ancient to me, a nineteen year old. Our job was to be the maintenance of the bridging equipment, while the greater part of the company was concerned with driving and maintaining the trucks that carried the equipment.

We soon got to know each other, and in a pub one evening Metcalfe and I discovered that we both liked singing, and for many songs he could sing the tenor part while I sang the air in a baritone key. We sang most of the way back from the pub, when we weren't talking about people and places we both knew. The company was soon mobile, and moved to Shirehampton, between Bristol and Avonmouth. There we parked in the streets, off the main road. We slept in the trucks, but food and ablutions and other services were organized at the local recreation ground. The townspeople were very kind to us. After a few days, we, the sappers that is, marched to Avonmouth docks while the transport was being moved and loaded on to a ship. It was raining, and there were very few bystanders to watch us. I remember wondering, as we made our way through the depressing docks in our sodden greatcoats, if it was anything like this in the last war. We must have looked the same - tin hats, webbing pouches on each breast, Lee Enfield rifles at the slope.

In the Bristol Channel we were a small group of ships, hardly a convoy, plus several destroyers with their signal lights flashing and their coloured signalling flags constantly changing. They circled the freighters and dashed between them, making whoop-whoop noises. Metcalfe and I found a seat near the stern, watching the log spinning. I had visualised a convoy as a pretty staid affair, but these ships, heaving about in a choppy sea, with the destroyers weaving at speed and slicing through wave tops in clouds of spray, were very exhilarating to watch.

When evening came, we found a corridor where we could stretch out and sleep, and in the morning we watched the ship being docked at St. Nazaire. The old soldiers tried out their bits of French on the dockworkers while we awaited the order to disembark. Eventually we piled into the trucks, which had been unloaded before us, and the company made its way eastwards to a village near Le Mans called Neuville-sur-Sarthe. We were there just over a week, and met a number of villagers. One evening we met Monsieur and Madame Marteau in the village estaminet (café/bar) and they took three of us to their home for fried potato chips, and we brought some beer. This was the first occasion I had spent time with French people inside their own home, and I found it interesting and enjoyable, if not a little unusual. Our hosts were obviously in love, very much in love, or were all young French couples so demonstrative in front of people they had only just met? Madam was a schoolteacher at a local école, and Monsieur was a clerk who commuted daily to Le Mans. The conversation of all five of us was animated and quite wide-ranging. They kept a number of large bound reference books, and didn't hesitate to bring one to the table and search it avidly to clear up a point that had been raised. We also found a certain charm in the way they would exchange soulful looks while absentmindedly continuing in the general conversation, this usually culminating in a long and tender or even passionate kiss.

One book they referenced was technical and medical and included quite explicit diagrams, which they did not hesitate to discuss in detail. Our only regret that evening was that our command of the French language was so inadequate. Nevertheless it was an occasion to remember. We met other very friendly villagers. Two girls took Metcalfe and me around some extensive orchards. An old lady called from her garden and gave us more apricots than we could carry. On Sunday the fine old stone church was well attended, and the elderly ladies were dressed in black except for their peculiar white-starched, wing-shaped head coverings. They all greeted the British soldiers in a friendly manner.

All too soon we were on the road again, always heading east. At one roadside halt, two young ladies were amused at our efforts to speak French, and the older one produced a violin and played, "Cour lapin cour ..." (run rabbit) while they sang, and then offered us small apricots pickled in apricot brandy. We really appreciated this kind hospitality, recognizing that they knew we were journeying and would probably never see them again. These east-going roads were often cobbled, and sometimes straight as far as the eye could see. At one stop we were beside a huge orchard, and after stretching our legs a number of men started taking apples. Then a man in a pony-trap drove along the road and stopped at the farmhouse. He went inside and came out with a large basket, collected apples from the same trees and then made his way along the convoy, offering apples to everybody. I climbed into the back of a truck, not being prepared to face him, even though I hadn't robbed his trees.

Later we stopped for the night further along the road. The thoroughfare was wide, the ditch full of deep grass, and I could imagine myself snuggling in it, rolled in a blanket. Metcalfe and I strolled along the road before settling down, and came upon a farmyard. The farmer came towards us, his clogs rattling on the cobbled yard. We greeted him as best we could, and with a sudden thought asked if we could sleep against his haystack. He immediately pulled down armfuls of hay, warning us not to smoke, "Pas fumez!" (we thought he meant, "What nice perfume!") and asked us at what time did we want waking? We told him, and settled down. He called us very early, and invited us into his house. There were four rooms in a line, all whitewashed and thatched. Grapevines were trained along the front, and inside his wife was making coffee over a stone hearth with a fire made of sticks from the hedgerow. We all sat. She pressed us to eat, meanwhile pouring coffee into pint-sized bowls. There was a fragrant smell of the long sticks of fresh bread combined with wood smoke and coffee. There was butter in another basin, and sweet green grapes on the table, and under another upturned basin a chunk of green Camembert cheese. We chatted happily, about the news, about the war. He pulled out faded photographs, and some were of his father in uniform in WWI. All too soon we had to go, and we said goodbye in the morning sunshine. Their sunburned faces were smiling.

At the convoy, the rest of the sappers were moving, washing, shaving. The breakfast was cold tinned pilchards in tomato sauce. We ate that too. At our next stop, a squad was instructed to go by truck with an RASC driver to collect rations. We went to the edge of a small town and found our objective, some recently requisitioned buildings including a few dwelling houses. There was a local sentry on a rooftop, and so I had my first look at a poilu (French infantry soldier, especially one who had fought in WWI). He wore a neat helmet that struck a chord - it was classic - right out of the page of a history book. His greatcoat was quite long and two corners were folded back from the front and buttoned, as were another two corners folded from the back vent and similarly buttoned. He wore puttees very similar to the British, just as they were in the First War and right up to 1938, and he carried a rifle with a vicious looking bayonet that was long and tapering, finishing with a point like a knitting needle. He had obviously noted our interest, and struck a pose, surveying the landscape. We were smiling as we entered.

Another French soldier, expecting us, took us to different rooms where we drew the various rations. We took cheeses, each two-feet across and nine-inches thick, and round black rye loaves, and carried out very large hunks of beef from the pieces and quarters which were piled on the floors of a number of the ground floor rooms, plus other items like flour, sugar and so on. There was nothing wrong with the meat, but it was very bloody, as were the floors, so I didn't fancy beef for a day or so... but soon got over that. When we were issued with the black bread and cheese at a meal, I heard some fellows making mock groans, but I enjoyed the food, particularly the cheese that had a very satisfying and slightly astringent taste.

Ultimately we arrived at a small town called Corbie in the Somme river valley, and were quartered in various locations. An empty building became the company office, and an adjoining structure was used to house the RE detachment. Our building had probably been a warehouse, and Sergeant Gray and a staff sergeant called Langton took what had been an office at one end of it. We sappers were quite crowded, but soon settled in and were glad to be under a roof after enduring some very makeshift sleeping arrangements. We didn't know it then, but this was to be our home for the next half year. The company office faced the largest square in the town, a square of dirt with a few trees, surrounded by an asphalt road. Behind the office building was a large garden, overgrown and with a few apple trees, and we could enter the garden via the office to get access to our quarters. At the end of our warehouse was a covered carriageway leading to a small lane, and in the carriageway was a narrow stairway leading to an attic.

Corbie (the name means raven) was a fine little town, 9 miles upriver from Amiens. It had grown up around an ancient abbey, founded by monks and influenced by Irish missionaries way back around 650 A.D. From the company office we could see the twin towers of the small but very attractive 18thC abbey church, only a stone's throw from the other side of the square. There were about seven or eight grocers' shops, a patisserie, a charcuterie (deli), a boucherie, a boucherie chevaline (horse butcher), a hairdresser salon, a watchmaker, ironmonger, blacksmith, and any number of bars and estaminets serving wine, beer and refreshments. The bridging trucks were parked mostly on a minor road that ran parallel with the River Somme, which hereabouts came from the north.

During those first days and weeks we met many of the locals. At the watchmaker's place, le patron taught me to say, "Voulez vous parlez plus lentement, s'il vous plait?" (Would you speak more slowly please?) The lady in the patisserie had known a British officer in WWI, and told many anecdotes about him, possibly thinking there was somebody who knew him. It was quite sad because she so obviously hoped for news of him. A lady in a haberdashery showed me a steel dart that she had recovered from a window shutter after a German plane had dropped thousands on the town. It was shaped and pointed at one end like a pencil, but the other end was deeply grooved to ensure it fell point first. A schoolteacher invited four of us to the local school and presented us to a class of eight-year olds. Not knowing quite what to do, one sapper asked if the class would sing the Marseillaise, which they readily did, and beautifully, and then of course he asked if we would sing God save the King, which we did in return.

We subsequently found out that our arrival had initiated the opening of numerous estaminets, many people furnishing a front room (or maybe two rooms) with a bar, chairs and tables. This had inevitably resulted in price hikes, and so we were unpopular with some locals, but for the most part we were well liked. The rate of exchange was about 170 francs to 1 pound sterling. Many sappers and drivers were earning two shillings a day, or slightly more. If they were tradesmen, as I was, they made about three shillings and nine pence. So my pay was equivalent to approximately 32 francs a day, and in most estaminets a dish of egg and chips cost just 3 francs. Beer was cheap too, and although initially the men considered it 'onion water' when compared to English beer, we soon got to like it.

Metcalfe and I tried many estaminets, and on entering one we saw biftec and chips chalked on the board, so we asked for it. It was very good, but the meat was sweetish and had a different but not unpleasant flavour. We mentioned this to la patronne, Madame Renee, who told us with a charming smile that the steaks came from the boucherie chevaline next door. That boucherie had a gilded horse's head figurine over the entrance, and on Saturdays a real, tired, old looking horse would usually be tethered outside. Although I had never consciously thought about it before, it was probably dispatched and butchered at the back of the shop. The front windows were often full of meat products: joints, bowls of minced meat and various shapes and sizes of sausages.

Le forgeron (the blacksmith) was quite near the billet, so we often greeted the farrier (horse cobbler) who was invariably friendly. He was short, stocky, and had a severe outward cast in one eye. The first time I met him he took me through to the kitchen, introduced me to his wife and daughter (an attractive, muscular, seventeen year old) and poured liqueur glasses of kirsch. He rolled his own cigarettes. The lighter was on the wall - two corrugated strips of brass wired with 110v electricity. Hanging near them was a small bottle with a wick protruding through a brass tube. He stroked the corrugated brass pieces with the tube and the resulting sparks ignited the wick.

One day he asked our blacksmith corporal to help him, and I looked in on them later in the morning. They were working in the centre of the shop, which was huge, mostly in shadow, and there were several dim electric light bulbs, their hanging wires disappearing into the darkness above. The boss was holding a massive piece of white-hot steel with two tongs, and his daughter and the corporal were each swinging a sledge. Their intent faces were lit from below with the glowing steel and the coals. The quick regular blows of the sledges sent showers of sparks upwards and tremors shook the floor. There was an air of quiet confidence about each of them, the girl with a slight smile on her handsome face as she intently watched her father for the slight nod that preceded each blow; the tall corporal with his firm chin and confident steady eyes; the boss intently studying the steel as its incandescent shape slowly changed. I was entranced and thought, "This is something to remember." After a while I stole away quietly, and as I walked a tremor seemed to move the very sidewalk with each regular thump from the forge.

The river Somme passed through the town to the east of our billet, about three hundred yards away, and there was a disused coal yard, with some old buildings, right next to a towpath. The company had utilised this yard as a park for vehicles carrying miscellaneous stores, and a guard was stationed on site nightly. Metcalfe was now a corporal, and took his turn as a guard commander, along with myself usually present. We learned to say, "Halt! Qui va la?" to any civilian who approached, but were quite unsure how to respond to a stream of rapid French in reply. We had a small wood stove in one building, so we soon made ourselves comfortable. One of the guards had lost a clip of five rounds of ammunition, and we all spent a lot of time vainly trying to find it.

Out of the darkness the sentry on duty called "Corporal Metcalfe - a couple of ladies here to see you." It was Marie with Monique. We had enjoyed a drink with them in Marie's estaminet only yesterday, and among other things had told them about this guard duty, and so the darlings had decided to surprise us with a visit! We hoped that the orderly officer wouldn't take it into his head to visit the coal yard. Asking the sentry to keep watch for us, we opened an adjoining building where straw was stored, and settled down to see what the girls had in their baskets. They had brought two thermos flasks full of coffee, biscuits, dainty sandwiches, and a bottle of brandy with four glasses! We started a most unusual guard session, eating and drinking and cuddling there in the dim building, lit only by the reflected light from a storm lantern and the stove next door. Just as the activity in the near darkness got to a really interesting stage there was a loud crack! One of the lost rounds had exploded. Talk about quick thinking! We dashed out shouting to the sentry and the off-duty guards to get well away from the stove. The girls meanwhile retreated to a safe side of the buildings - just in time because the rest of the rounds started to explode and some loose straw went up in flames. We kept clear until all five rounds went off, and then set about beating out the flames.

We looked for the girls, but they had disappeared. That was probably just as well because a man had been walking his dog along the towpath and the howling and barking added to the din, bringing out a group of interested spectators from the nearby café, so our rendezvous with the girls would have been observed. Next morning the guard was 'stood down' at 0630 hours, and they all went back to the billets except for Metcalfe and me. We went into an estaminet - Le Café a la Descent de la Marine - where we had hot grog that the patron was particularly good at making. He would put a tot of Rhum Negrita in a glass, adding hot water, and then a quick squirt from each of six different bottles. Santé!

As the months went by I got to know the sappers, and some of the locals too. One tall sapper called Satchwell had a very cultured accent and said he had been in management at a Walls Ice Cream factory. Some didn't believe him, and several rib-poking wags took any opportunity to call out "Wallzay!" at him from a distance. They also rumoured, in that fondness among certain troops to make fun of a man who was well spoken, that he had in fact merely sold ice cream from a tricycle. Many of the townspeople were very friendly, and were often ready to chat, or at least pass the time of day. There was the barber who taught me to say, "Voulez vous couper mes cheveux?" In France your hairs are plural, not singular, as in the word 'fur' for example.

Sergeant Gray surprised us all one day by appearing at reveille clad only in a shirt and with a storm lantern swinging from his private member, a feat widely acclaimed because no one could understand how he kept his appendage rigid enough to support such a weight! Then there was a fat sapper, Jennings, one of a pair who did the detachment's cooking. When the notion took him, he would appear to wind himself up standing on one leg and make strange and funny noises that were quite hilarious, some almost unbelievable, requiring considerable muscle control. He then concluded this performance by bowing and smiling coyly. Savage was another sapper, an electrician, who could be quite amusing. He was forever joking, and told us that this had got him into trouble. He was once wiring a bathroom and noticed that the lavatory seat was polished hardwood fitted with brass hinges. He wired the seat so that the hinges were earthed via the water in the pan if the circuit was completed by someone urinating. The lady of the house used the toilet, with the result that our man was fired on the spot. Or at least that was his story. He was quite a good tradesman, and rewired the blacksmith's entire forge while refusing any payment.

In the billet, Sergeant Gray gave out the mail and most men gathered in happy anticipation. I noticed that one of the oldest sappers, Sherwell, never bothered. One night, while doing a guard duty with him, he told me that he had no relatives. Not sadly, just matter of fact. He had no hair either, and no teeth. He had travelled to various medical centres for a denture fitting, or repair, or modification. Some claimed that he spent his whole time searching northern France for suitable dentures.

In one of my mother's letters, she asked me if there were any men in the detachment who received no mail from home, so I gave her Sherwell's name. When I next received a parcel from home, he got one as well, exactly the same. It contained chocolates and cakes, and especially coconut haystacks: small cakes made with eggs, sugar and shredded coconut. Sherwell came around straight away, and I've never seen a man so moved, near to tears, as he tried to say that he was about to write a thank-you letter to my mother.

Some time later it was announced that we would get home leave, and Sergeant Gray wrote dates on pieces of paper that were put into a hat, and we each drew one. I and an older man called Raithby, from Brigg in Lincolnshire, were the lucky ones, having drawn dates covering Christmas. Immediately Sapper Savage offered me four thousand francs if I would change dates with him. This equated to nearly twenty-four pounds sterling, a handsome offer for which I thanked him but declined to accept it. Several men complained that married men with children should get the Christmas break, but did not pursue this. The weeks passed, and my day of departure came. When going on leave, a man took his complete kit - rifle, bayonet, kitbag, greatcoat, tin hat, pack and haversack - the lot! This was in case our unit got moved while we were on leave. I was packing when Sherwell came and invited me to have a farewell drink at Madame Gabby's, so off we went. Raithby came too. Madame Gabby was about sixty, a bit shorter than average, and fairly plump, but quite an attractive lady. She dressed well, had a wonderful bosom, which she 'made the most of', and her deportment was superb. She wore pince-nez spectacles, and although she did not speak English, she was very quick on the uptake.

When Sherwell approached her and started to whisper in a conspiratorial manner, she adopted a grave countenance, with a theatrical expression denoting that her cooperation and understanding were complete and total. She disappeared into the cellar and re-emerged with a fine bottle of champagne that was covered with cobwebs! With great ceremony she presented the bottle and uncorked it, a loud pop snapping as the cork flew off and hit the ceiling, exactly where she so obviously knew it would. Then she poured each glass while saying a few words to the person for whom it was poured. Without seeming to try, she had turned Sterling's farewell drink into an occasion, and we responded. Sherwell proposed a toast - to The King. We then toasted the President of France, the British army, the French army, and we said lots of nice things about everybody we could possibly think of, our families at home, and the people of the town.

I thought it was time we had another bottle, and yet it wasn't very long before Raithby thought another was needed, and then it wasn't long before I slipped on to the floor and Gabby was tickling me where she shouldn't have. Others had crowded into the estaminet, and they and the waitress, and of course Gabby, were proposing courses of action. They all knew that I would soon have to attend a pay parade, and the puzzle was how to get me to behave normally. I don't remember all the remedies, but I do remember the washing soda (sodium carbonate or soda ash). They had mixed up a solution of washing soda and water, and having taken it I thought I was going to die. There ensued an agony of retching, alternating with pairs of men 'helping' me to walk up and down. Soon I was standing in a queue of men with Raithby - the rest being RASC - and when my name was called, I replied, "Surp!" and marched smartly forward until I struck the pay table with my thighs and hit the ledger with my hands. As everything slid towards the pay officer, I found myself staring into his eyes at close range. "Pull yourself together man!" he barked. But he paid me, bless him, and shortly afterwards Raithby and I were sitting on wooden slat seats in a local train clattering towards Amiens. We found that we had to wait some time for a connecting train to the port of Boulogne.

We walked for a while in the dark streets, and then entered a French military canteen. It was crowded with French poilus, and included a group of Algerian spahis (ceremonial cavalry guards) in their colourful cloaks. We found seats at a table, there being no counter as in a British canteen, and were waited on by a soldier. I asked for two coffees, which seemed to throw him, but then he departed. The place was almost dark, with a near solid cloud of smoke from scores of Gauloise cigarettes, the wires from the bare lamp bulbs disappearing into the gloom above. The poilus were curious about us, and we were curious about them. Quite a few of them spoke a little English, and with our bits of French we started conversation. The coffee arrived (I suspect from a neighbouring café) but we soon had to depart, somewhat regretfully, because both Raithby and I felt that it had been a good contact.

We shouldered our rifles and left, walking to the station where we collected the rest of our kit and shortly thereafter boarded our train. There were troops from many regiments, each man festooned with equipment like us. We lay or sat where we could and tried to sleep as the night wore on, an untidy mixture of men, kit bags, rifles, packs and tin hats. We arrived in Boulogne in the early morning, organized into squads and marched to the top of a steep hill where a transit camp had been established. We queued for a bacon sandwich and tea, and were then herded into huts where each of us selected a bed comprising a straw-filled palliase (thin mattress) laid on three planks that were supported on short wooden trestles. It was okay - actually very welcome on a dark, rainy winter's morning.

Eventually we turned out and marched to the docks where we boarded a ship, and I experienced my worst channel crossing ever. I couldn't possibly have stayed below, but up on top it was also pretty awful. Spray was blowing about all over the heaving deck, and the occasional wave came right across it, spewing quantities of water deep enough to move kitbags and other gear. Many soldiers just didn't care, myself included! At long last we reached Dover and a train took us to Waterloo station in London, where we walked out to the main concourse to find a large crowd waiting. The lucky ones were greeted by their loved ones, and I noted two well-fed, well-dressed gentlemen who made it obvious they were there to help. It was noticeable that soldiers kept clear of them. Raithby and I wished each other well. I headed for Paddington station to travel southwest and he went north to Lincolnshire.

Arriving at Camborne in Cornwall I was met by my brother-in-law Irving, and on the way home I listened to his accounts of his efforts to join a navy, either royal or merchant. The problem was that he was in a reserved occupation and the authorities always blocked his attempts. He had two brothers and two cousins in the Royal Navy, a sister married to an officer in the merchant navy, and his wife had a brother in the RAF and another in the army - me - but there was no such service for him.

I had a wonderful leave, with my father, mother, sister and Irving making it an occasion. All too soon I was standing again on Camborne station, lugging rifle, kit bag, pack and tin hat, about to retrace my steps back to the small French town of Corbie in the Somme river valley.

We were in Corbie right through the winter of 1939-40 and it was bitterly cold. During one cold snap we experienced snow frequently alternating with rain and hard frost. The streets and sidewalks were almost impassable, especially on foot. People grabbed at windowsills for support, but it was hazardous between them. The road surface was a series of humps and pits, and just like glass overall. At the billet, Metcalfe and I, and half a dozen others, had moved up into the attic. An old printing press and bits of office furniture were smothered in dust and littered the place, so we cleared a way through and found a reasonably sound floor at the far end, furthest from the stairway. We divided this area off with a screen of hessian tacked to studwork. Our first beds were straw palliasses laid on the floor, but we improved on this by scrounging enough timber to make frame beds, laced across the top with old leather belting that we found in a disused factory.

One evening I had returned through the icy streets to the billet intending to turn in. I climbed the stairs and made my way across the rickety floor, and saw the 'night commode', a three-gallon tin can that we used for urination. Right above it was a skylight, and the rule was that if you found the container full, then it was your turn to empty it. To perform this you raised the (by now) quite heavy container and tipped it so that it emptied through the skylight, which was a little higher than a man's head. You had to be careful or you finished the job with wet sleeves, or worse. The urine then coursed down the tiles with a rushing, gurgling noise that one could hear from inside, ran along the lead gutter to a vertical iron down-pipe, disappeared below the cobbled carriageway entrance and finally emerged in an open drain near the RASC cookhouse. Carefully standing on this container, I found that I could push my head and shoulders through the skylight, which was about two feet by one foot. I gazed right across the town. All its roofs, dominated by the twin church towers, were covered in snow and looked silver in the moonlight. It was all a vibrant pale blue with deep purple in the shadows.

I scrambled through the skylight and slid down the pantiles to the gutter. Then, feeling at peace with the world, I stood and serenaded the town with, "One night I lay adreaming..." while walking along the leaded gutter. After a few more songs like, "Hurrah for the Cornish floral dance..." and "J'attendrais..." I slipped on the lumpy snow, fell right off the roof and dropped atop a lean-to, rolled off that and fell into a garden, my head having broken a clothesline, which skinned my ear. I lay in the snow while the clothesline sprang back and twanged on a window - the kitchen window of Madame Gabby's estaminet. She and a waitress came rushing out with cries of alarm and dragged me into their kitchen, where they checked me over, prodding the most likely and unlikely places, while forcing cognac into my willing mouth. Ultimately, they helped me up and walked me to the back door of my billet. I finally got to bed feeling no worse, in fact somewhat better, for my experience.

Then there was Victor, an ancient local who sold rabbit skins that he had cured. I was told that he was one of the few remaining vendors because the demand for such skins for use in dressmaking was declining. Victor invariably wore an alpine beret, but his was like a small roof and he peered out from one end that was folded like a gable. His trousers were too short, exposing bare ankles and feet that were thrust into clogs lined with straw. Over his left arm he carried a pile of skins, and with his right hand he grasped a stick. He would pause at the edge of the sidewalk and shout a stream of unintelligible patois ending suddenly with, "...poh!" (peaux meaning skins). If he did this while the company was preparing to parade in the main square, the troops would give him a cheer, to which he would respond by giving the company a good scolding, waving his stick at us.

Generally our interaction with the townspeople was good, and I don't remember any complaints of bad behaviour - well, only one anyway. The town had generously informed us that we could use the swimming pool free of charge during the mornings. The first group to go swimming had, I suppose, assumed that this meant in the nude, thinking we wouldn't be expected to possess swim shorts. This outraged the townspeople, and the privilege was immediately withdrawn. But, throughout our stay there, the town did let us use their playing fields for soccer and hockey games, and often the townspeople were spectators. One time I remember a man with his wife and two daughters watching a game when he turned away from them and relieved himself on the open field. The French people there seemed concerned only because they saw the looks of astonishment on the British faces.

Most of us failed to learn more than a few words of French, myself being one of the exceptions. I could remember a little French from my days at secondary school and I thought it worthwhile to learn a bit more. My copy of Hugo's French Verbs had a foldout section where the irregular verbs were tabulated, and I had pinned this to the attic ceiling close above my bed. I made strenuous efforts to master them, and on a Friday I would try out some of them on the market traders and their customers. But frequently the stream of rapid French in the replies was completely unintelligible. The Somme patois was particularly difficult. An old chap like Victor might well say, "Cammank shah voh?" for example, instead of, "Comment ca va?" (How are you?)

The market stalls were put up on the main square, and were the usual mix of bona fide regular traders and a few 'wide boys' (wheeler-dealers) selling knick-knacks. They were invariably good-natured, with a nod and a smile for our troops who generally bought next to nothing. British chaps couldn't fail to note that the French were polite anyway, always using the terms monsieur, madam and mam'selle. Monsieur meant more than "mister" - it meant "Sir!"

We continued playing hockey and soccer. Metcalfe and I had singing lessons from a Monsieur Camus from the Amiens Conservatoire de Musique. We had come to know him because he gave clarinet lessons to a French acquaintance of ours. We also got to know our comrades in arms even better. Sergeant Gray came from Kent, and claimed that he was an inspector on the buses. 'Dolly' had lost all the teeth in his upper jaw except one, an incisor that was very large. He had a nervous habit of chewing on nothing, and the incisor had worn a deep curve in his lower teeth. One fun-making wag reckoned that 'Dolly' had really been a bus or train conductor, and had used this tooth for punching tickets.

The long months spent in Corbie were hardly exciting. The bridging equipment was well maintained and held ready for eventualities, and was sometimes used for training by the various engineer companies in northern France. We made efforts to amuse ourselves. When the Somme was frozen, a few of us tried skating. Metcalfe and I were invited to a number of singing functions held by neighbouring units. Also our own company put a concert party together and staged a show. A few French people performed, including a very fine baritone who sang, "On ne pas..." The closing item was a darkened scene with a solitary man tending a campfire while he hummed a tune. Twos and threes joined him until there was a small choir. Then the party slowly diminished as ones and twos waved goodnight, until the last solitary figure put out the fire. This gave us the scope to include every would-be singer, and was very popular. At one performance, a brigadier was in the audience, and he helped us as an unofficial conductor during the campfire scene by waving the end of his glowing cigar in time with the various songs.

But things were to change in the spring.

Chapter 2

It was in early April 1940 that German forces had entered several Norwegian ports, and we were aware that the Royal Navy with the Fleet Air Arm had attacked their ships returning to Germany, sinking some of them. The British and French also landed forces in Norway in mid-April. We in the Bridge Company knew something of this, not that we could understand much in a French newspaper apart from working out what the headlines meant. We had moved out from Corbie, eventually to be stationed further northeast in France, to provide a bridging service when required by the BEF, the bulk of the British Army in Europe at the time.

The British Expeditionary Force constituted one tenth of the Allied forces in Europe and was deployed across the French-Belgian border area, along with the French, in readiness to counter any German aggression. Together, the British and French were known as the Western Allies. But during these months no initiative or commitment was made by any western power to launch a significant offensive against Germany, despite the fact that the enemy had already overrun Poland in a mere 5 weeks, and as a result both England and France had formally declared war on Germany. This period of non-action against the growing threat was to become known as the 'Phoney War' or, to use Churchill's description of it, the 'Twilight War'. The Polish called it the 'Strange War', and the French referred to it as the 'Joke War'.

However, at the time, we in the ranks were poorly briefed. We simply knew that we were moving north and assumed that the whole army was as well. Sporadically we saw German planes, usually two or three, including 'Pencil Dorniers' and other medium bombers, and occasionally a small reconnaissance plane. No British planes. We were travelling in convoy with the usual problems. The whole company was spread out, attempting to keep to 'target spacing' between trucks. This enabled other users - not that there were many - to freely use the road - to be overtaken or overtake us without hindrance. At times the leading vehicle would for some unknown reason be unable to keep to the target speed. The next vehicle would then catch up a little and the distance between them would be shortened. This effect would be repeated throughout the convoy, the cumulative effect being so marked that vehicles near the end of the convoy would actually have to stop for minutes at a time, sometimes for thirty or even forty.

Meanwhile, the leading vehicle would resume target speed, and the following unit would emulate it as soon as the driver was aware of this. Invariably he would be a little late in so doing, and the distance between them would increase, so he would increase speed to correct the interval. The whole procession would again be disrupted, progressively worsening towards the rear. For drivers at the latter end of a convoy this would be very frustrating. It was quite common for their advancement during a long journey to consist of high-speed spurts alternating with periods where progress was reduced to a crawl with frequent stops. At the end of one such day the company was near the town of Marchiennes, where we halted and the vehicles were split up into groups and parked in fields and along hedgerows. We had seen a number of enemy planes during the day but had not ourselves been attacked. We spent the evening cutting brushwood to add to the scrim nets used for camouflage, working until darkness fell. We sat around for a while, yarning before turning in. I was with a small group of vehicles on a hilltop, most of us being sappers, with three drivers who were attached to us.

The small fields and thick hedgerows reminded me of Cornwall, and reminded Bert Oliver too. Bert was an RASC driver who also came from Cornwall. He was short and dark - and invariably had a bottle of beer around him somewhere! He drove a brewery wagon before joining up, delivering barrels and bottles to pubs. Every landlord offered Bert a pint, and he always accepted. As a consequence he had developed an incredible capacity. He also retained a fund of risqué stories, and was inevitably a popular character. And he looked the part, with his twinkling dark eyes and ready laugh. He wore his forage cap centrally and aligned fore and aft, with the central crease slightly open. His greatcoat was far too big, almost sweeping the ground. I sometimes helped him drink a bottle before we turned in.

In the morning some of the men set to cutting more brushwood. Corporal Giblin (another sapper) and I went with a driver in the 'fish van' to a vehicle park in the valley, where some of the pontoon trucks were located. This fish van, as we called it, did not look like a military vehicle at all. It was painted a matt khaki, and had the usual divisional signs, but it still looked like a fish van! We travelled with the rear door open, where the two of us sat with our legs dangling close to the ground. In the valley we had reached a long straight part of the road leading south when we saw a medium bomber flying low. It was immediately obvious that it would overtake us in a matter of seconds. We yelled a warning to the driver who pulled over as fast as possible and we all sprinted into a farmyard. We dashed to a small door in an outbuilding and found ourselves in a toilet, just as the plane roared overhead and a stick of bombs started blasting off. I found myself staring at Corporal Giblin, from a range of seven inches, as with each bomb his eyes widened further, and his jaw dropped more. I didn't exactly laugh, more like a barking noise, while the building was shaking and a crack opened up before us. Then the plane was gone and all was quiet as the three of us disentangled our limbs and burst out. There were five evenly spaced craters, two before the farmyard and three beyond it. No casualties, and no building or vehicle damage to speak of. If there were any people at the farm, they were well hidden.

We carried on to the vehicle park, which was a field with maybe a dozen or more trucks each loaded with two pontoons or pontooning equipment, tucked in close to the hedgerows and covered with scrim netting. There were bomb craters everywhere, some very large - twenty to thirty feet across - but no truck had received a direct hit. We were joined by another squad of sappers and were examining the equipment when there was another raid. Again a number of bombers came from the north, quite low in the sky. We scattered, and I found myself in a small crater with another sapper. He was fumbling for something, and I was amazed to see him produce a cork, which he placed between his teeth! He was a north countryman called Nessing, a reservist and quite a plump fellow. I stared at him and tried to remember something that I had heard about this use of corks, and then we could hear the whistle of bombs. Again I became a bit hysterical. Nessing's eyes were protruding from his smooth moon face, looking really surprised, with the cork holding his teeth apart. Fear formed a knot in my belly while the bombs were crashing around us. I have often wondered what I must have looked like. Suddenly it was over, and there were men emerging from all sorts of hidey-holes. Again, amazingly, no one was hurt. Nessing immediately started talking. "The cork," he said, "keeps the mouth open and thereby protects the eardrums from the pressure waves emanating from the explosions, because the small spaces on either side of the cork in the mouth ensure equal atmospheric pressure on either side of each eardrum." It was a learned dissertation delivered in a gentle Yorkshire accent.

Back at the hilltop we found that they too had been bombed, but again, no one was hurt and no trucks were hit directly. The camouflage had been much improved by the time they were raided, and we wondered how much difference that had made. We learned that Bert had suffered a bad fright, so I went to look for him. He showed me a huge tree where he had been cutting branches, and beside it was a crater that could easily have held a big bridging truck. "I was up the tree," he said, "when they came. I got halfway down when the bomb hit. I was blown off on to the grass and covered in dirt. I couldn't move or speak for a while." He grinned at me, but the hand holding the cigarette was shaking.

Yarning about it that evening, everyone felt it was incredible that there were no casualties, and those of us who had been in the fish van were amazed that a bomber would target such a small isolated vehicle. We talked of incidents that had occurred before we arrived at Marchiennes, in various places west of where we were now stopped. We had been machine-gunned by Dorniers while waiting at the roadside. Bullets had hit pontoon trucks, penetrating both pontoons, which were carried in pairs, and had finished up in the undercarriage or in the road below. Meanwhile the drivers had taken cover away from the road. Elsewhere we had stopped momentarily, and there, at a crazy angle, was a wrecked military ambulance. A group of us, me included, had sprinted across to see if anything could be done. A dead soldier lay on a stretcher on the grass nearby. The ambulance had obviously been abandoned. The soldier's belongings had been taken as well as one identity tag, the other being left round his neck. The convoy was moving again, so we sprinted back.

Two RASC men described how they had taken cover during a raid while other units nearby had opened up with ack-ack and shot down one of the bombers. These fellows had dashed across to the wrecked plane and pulled one man clear before the wreckage burst into flames. The German was conscious but badly injured and had asked for a cigarette. "An English one, please," he had said with a grin. A truck then took him away to find medical help.

On one stretch of road we were joined by a stream of refugees, and for most of the day experienced continuous delays. We tried to give them unhindered passage, but it was very difficult. They were of all ages, and moving slowly. They carried various containers holding their belongings, ranging from small bundles carried in their hands to large trunks balanced on their shoulders or carried in a wheelbarrow. One old man was pushing a wheelbarrow with an old lady sitting on it, perched atop a huge assortment of belongings. Husband and wife, I thought. There were also pony traps and heavy farm wagons, and one car was pulled by a horse. A mattress had been tied across the roof of the car to provide some protection against shrapnel. Some refugees were well dressed, some very poorly, and all looked completely dejected.

One morning a group of about eight of us were sent to complete a bridging project that another unit had started. We arrived to find a folding boat bridge across a canal. Only a few girders and decking were needed, so we set to it. We were told that this bridge was to divert the refugee traffic; thereby keeping the roads clear for the military. After a short while a spotter plane (similar to our own Auster aircraft) started circling over a point to the northwest of us. Thinking our activity might result in a bombing raid, we retired into an isolated roadside cafe on the canal bank and from there watched the plane for a while. Our transport had returned to the company, so from the air the site would appear deserted. Our captain arrived by car and asked why the delay, and our corporal explained. The captain stared at him, and then stared at us. After that he turned and walked towards the bridge, picked up a deck plank and laid it, talking all the while quite softly. One of the things he said was, "You must have faith." The captain was, to us, quite elderly, with WWI ribbons, including that of the Belgian Croix de Guerre. The spotter plane was still circling. He went back for another deck plank.

"Come on chaps," the corporal said, and we worked with a will until the bridge was finished. Then we stood by the cafe waiting for our transport, the elderly captain having long gone. A motorcycle came from the east along the canal bank road, and pulled up beside us. The rider wore an RE cap badge, and had a greatcoat on, which seemed a bit strange in the warm sunshine. He had no badges of rank, and asked if the road led to Dunkirk. No one was sure, but we thought it did. He roared off. Suddenly I remembered him, the sergeant I had seen from the classroom window when the course was cancelled for the second time at the School of Military Engineering in Chatham. And this time I remembered his name - it was

Cassel. A truck arrived and took us back to our unit, at which point it was parked among the hedgerows. We hadn't seen any refugees on the various roads near the bridge.

From then on we were moving, under instructions, and each move brought us ever nearer to Dunkirk. Before we left the Marchiennes district, groups of us were designated to destroy pontoon and other equipment trucks. Nothing that was usable was to fall into enemy hands. Unknown to me, a number of folding boats were moved to the Dunkirk area. No information whatsoever about enemy movements reached us, from our superiors or from anyone else. We learned much later that enemy armour was using the roads immediately west of Marchiennes, and to the southeast, hence the intense air activity over our area and our own parked equipment.

Travelling westwards, we saw aircraft and were subjected to some strafing, but not to the same extent as in the Marchiennes area. At one place, spread out on some open farm land, we could see French gunners positioning their guns, towing them using half-tracks. This was the first and only time I had seen half-tracks, vehicles steered by rubber-tired wheels in the front, while the main power is provided by tracks, like a tank. I don't think the tracks provided anything towards the steering. We also came across an abandoned canteen van where two soldiers were distributing goods to all and sundry. I was offered, and took, several hundred expensive cigarettes, which later proved very useful for bartering.

We became involved with more refugees when quite near Dunkirk. It was evening, so we avoided them by getting off the road and settling down for the night in a wood. The ground was quite flat for miles, and was crisscrossed by drainage ditches with some water in them. The water was faintly luminous for some reason. Also the air was alive with mosquitoes. When I settled down to sleep, I wrapped my greatcoat around my head and shoulders, leaving a small hole through which to breathe, but the mosquitoes still got through to me. I spent an uncomfortable night and awoke the next morning covered with mosquito bites. One eye was completely shut and the other nearly so. Metcalfe laughed like a drain - no sympathy there!

On the northeast side of Dunkirk there is a place called Bray-Dunes, and Metcalfe and I were mixed in with the scores of troops scattered across the dunes, looking down at the beach, which was maybe a mile away. From Dunkirk itself there was a pall of black smoke that covered half the sky. Imagine it, from one horizon to the other; half of the entire sky was smoke - brown and black rolling clouds of smoke that blotted out the afternoon sun. It came from the docks and was blown inland by an onshore wind. Close to the beach there were forty or more craft, most of them small apart from five or six freighters, one of which was wearing the Norwegian flag. A German fighter howled across the dunes with his guns chattering. Hundreds of rifles answered his fire, and several machine guns, two of them firing tracer. He was out of sight in seconds, and there were no casualties. We made our way to the town where several houses were smouldering and gutted. A medium twin-engine bomber appeared, flying eastwards low over the small boats along the coast. He held his course, ignoring the small-arms fire that met him. We stared fascinated as a cluster of small black shapes fell from him, falling so fast they became lost to view until suddenly the centre of a freighter erupted. By then the bomber was hugging the ground inland and disappearing rapidly. Flames and smoke were coming from the freighter, the one with the Norwegian flag.

We pressed on, entering a straight road that led to the sea front, and at the other end we could see a bandstand with uniformed figures around it. At a road junction a platoon of Scottish infantry was coming towards us, led by a kilted piper, and then a subaltern with a walking stick. We were stopped in our tracks, somewhat surprised, and greatly impressed. We sloped arms and saluted, feeling just a little bit silly, but we simply couldn't *not* salute! We waited until they were past, and then made our way to the beach beyond the bandstand, where we were ignored. After that we joined a queue, and stood there in the sand for the rest of the day, remaining there for all that night, and for part of the next morning. The men were incredibly quiet and well behaved. There was no queue jumping, and if a man left the queue to answer 'the call of nature' the remaining men protected his place. There were many queues, some immediately to the east of us, and many on both sides but further away.

On the first day a number of small boats were ferrying men out to the larger boats. There was a paddle steamer that someone from London recognized. During that evening very few men got off the beach. As it got darker it was very noticeable that the seawater was luminous, much more radiant than the water we had seen inland, a condition known as phosphorescence caused by disturbed micro-organisms. Wherever a man walked on the wet sand, each footmark glowed brightly, and he left behind a trail of a dozen or so footmarks still gleaming. The sea was calm, and at the waters edge the ripples broke in long lines of fire, one disappearing as another started.

As the night wore on we tried to doze while standing up, and occasionally a man fell over. Our position in the queue was a little below high tide mark, and the water came up to my knees before retreating. Most of the time my feet were apart and the butt of my rifle was in the sand while I held the muzzle against my midriff. Twice during that night we heard a shot, but little fuss was made. Everyone assumed that they were accidental.

In the morning there was greater activity than on the previous day. More boats were negotiating the small surf and taking men to larger craft. Near us, a naval officer was struggling alone to tow a string of such boats with a small motorboat, and repeatedly broke the towropes by gunning the motor each time he was ready to tow. He just could not get the hang of it. Eventually he succeeded and departed. Later, our turn came, and the boat that took us out was laid alongside a boarding net hanging from the side of a destroyer, the HMS Esk. We scrambled up, struggling with pack and rifle, and were then shepherded below. Shortly after, an NCO came looking for any one who wore the RE cap badge. He wanted men who could handle large folding boats, so Metcalfe and I joined a group that went back down the boarding nets, and each of us was allocated a boat. These boats, about twenty-four feet long and six-foot abeam, were equipped with four rowlocks for rowing and would usually be steered by another oar plied over a central fairlead. One competent oarsman could handle an empty boat alone, either sculling, with one oar resting in the stern fairlead, or using a pair of oars in rowlocks.

For most trips one had to row the empty boat through the small surf, keeping the craft at right angles to the waves. If a boat was allowed to swing broadside to the waves it rocked dangerously, being flat-bottomed, and could easily capsize. Once in shallow water it was a case of persuading soldiers to take their time, to prevent the boat from grounding, to get on board one at a time, and to disperse themselves evenly and thereby keep the craft trimmed level. They had to be told that a boat would only take sixteen men, and that four of them would be required to row. On one trip a rower was quite drunk, and smelled strongly of rum. He insisted on rowing at odds to the other three, making the boat turn quite fast in small circles and yawing violently when broadside to the waves.

My appeals to several NCOs to control him went unheeded, and I started to get frantic, until the chap in the next boat said, "Take it easy soldier!" It was a young sailor, I guessed about seventeen, with his bell-bottoms rolled up and his legs covered in tar. He was cheerfully grinning, in spite of the strafing further along the beach. My sense of panic suddenly disappeared! Eventually, after struggling with my steering oar, we got through the small surf near the beach, and on that trip I was very thankful to get a tow from a motorboat. After a couple more trips we were ordered on board the destroyer HMS Esk, and as we made our way below we heard an announcement, "Clear for action." But we heard nothing resembling action as we steamed away.

When next we came on deck we were in Dover harbour, with the ships docked three aside against the jetties. We scrambled across the decks and, leaving the harbour, had to pass the RMP (Royal Military Police) Redcaps who took each man's weaponry away from him! For a regular soldier to have his rifle taken away by anyone (except someone senior to him in his own unit) was quite unthinkable. A Redcap took my Lee Enfield and threw it to the top of a huge pile of rifles. I was mortified, and offended by such treatment.

A very languid looking officer, dressed formally in gleaming Sam-Browne belt and pressed uniform, not much older than myself, draped himself over a barrier formed out of a five barred gate and lectured us on how we were to be taken to a transit camp, and from there dispersed to our re-forming units. I glanced around at the faces of the couple of hundred troops gathered there, their khaki outfits scruffy and crumpled, their tired stolid faces betraying no emotion as they listened. What were their thoughts, I wondered? What were the officer's thoughts? We were a beaten army, with not a wounded man to be seen, and a pompous little Redcap had disarmed us.

We made our way to a Dover train, which left shortly afterward, and travelled westwards for an hour or so, and then stopped at a small station in the country where a group of WVS (Women's Voluntary Service) ladies were well organized with tea trollies. These smiling women served tea, greeting the men as if it was a picnic, and gave each of us a card on which we could write a brief message home. I wrote, "I am safe and well in England - 30th May 1940." We had time to think about the massive retreat in which we had been involved. We had spent only two days on the beach, and during that time had seen some enemy action, but we could not say he had been really active. We thought the action must have been elsewhere, and we must have been very fortunate. After all, we had seen no casualties, although there must have been some on the Norwegian freighter that was bombed.

Later we got off the train at Perham Down, a small village in Wiltshire on the edge of Salisbury Plain, about 30 miles west of Aldershot, and trucks took us to a tented camp. In the days that followed we sat on the grass in large groups and patiently waited while an elderly officer with two clerks studied lists at a table in the open air. A warrant officer mustered groups from the units, as indicated by the older officer, and these groups were conveyed, usually by train, to their appropriate regiments. We spent a couple of days at Perham Down, and I guess many thousands of men were sorted and dispatched from there. I had recognized the warrant officer from the first day. Again, it was Cassel.

I was sent north to Ripon in Yorkshire, with Corporal Metcalfe and a few other sappers from the bridge company detachment. On arrival there we found the whole detachment re-assembled. This was now a training unit for RE personnel, and the majority of them were not from the BEF. A sergeant called Steer was well known to me, since I had known him as a Lance Corporal in the training battalion at Chatham in early 1938. The staff at Ripon started to put us through a rigorous training schedule, and it soon became apparent that a significant number of them thought that we, coming from the BEF, needed some hard training to lick us into shape. After all, we had run away (!) although they were careful not to say so. Maybe we did need some square bashing (who doesn't?) but regarding demolitions, knots and lashings, map reading, bridging, watermanship and the like, we were already experts. And when it came to rifle shooting on the range, they were taken aback to discover that they could learn from us!

We were soon packed off back south to join the newly formed 6th Bridge Company RASC in Savernake Forest, Wiltshire. At that time there was much talk of a possible invasion. We didn't even have enough rounds of ammunition to issue ten to each man! In Savernake Forest we received cases of Molotov cocktails, which were buried because this was considered the safest way to store them until they should be needed in case of landings by enemy tanks. Poles were being set up in many open spaces and fields to deter landings by enemy glider-borne troops. Almost every man in the unit had come through Dunkirk, and if we had any feeling that the British public regarded us as a beaten army this was universally dispelled. The general feeling was rather that the BEF had been inadequately equipped and prepared for the Blitzkrieg of the Low Countries (German offensive through the Netherlands and Belgium) as it came to be known. The withdrawal through Dunkirk had been the correct action to take. It had been well organized and was highly successful for two reasons. Firstly, the incredible help from civilian small boat owners, coupled with the abnormally good weather. Secondly, the mysterious behaviour of an enemy that had not attacked us with significant strength during our withdrawal.

The British Expeditionary Force, along with French and Belgian troops, had been trapped by the Germans who then paused in their offensive at the ports of Boulogne and Calais. At the same time the remaining 40,000 men of the French First Army held off no less than seven German divisions (100,000 infantry and 800 tanks) at the inland city of Lille, delaying their advance toward the coast for four days. This siege (May 28–Jun 1), coupled with the German's own tactical lapse at the ports, provided the critical days during which British destroyers, helped by many hundreds of small merchant ships and pleasure boats, evacuated 98,000 men from the beaches and 240,000 from Dunkirk harbour. The whole rescue operation of the stranded soldiers, which was officially named Operation Dynamo, also rightfully came to be called the Miracle Of Dunkirk.

As time went on I was to discover, from a number of ex-boy soldiers and others, how they had fared in the withdrawal from France. It was said that of the men who gathered near Dunkirk, more than 90% were successfully evacuated, including 100,000 French forces. In addition, many thousands more used the ports of northern France and escaped safely. I heard of an uncle of mine, Sergeant Major Haycocks of the Hampshire Regiment, who was mentioned in despatches for the way he organized the withdrawal of his troops via Dieppe. Of the BEF, for every seven men that escaped via Dunkirk, one was left behind and captured, and sent on forced marches to Germany. Much later I heard from an ex-boy who had been taken captive and spent the entire war in Poland. Those prisoners were forced to work with inadequate food, clothing or shelter, and were even forbidden the use of a sidewalk if German troops were about. When in dire need, he was forced to beg for food from Polish housewives who could ill afford to help him. He developed a hatred for Germany, and all things German, which stayed with him always.

Also later, I heard about the ship Lancastrian, which had embarked from St. Nazaire in western France loaded with troops, and after passing Ushant island and entering the English Channel had been bombed. Sapper Hutchison, an ex-boy who had joined the army with me years before, was among the many who scrambled on to the keel as the ship turned over. He described how the unsteady hull was settling in an oil-covered sea, with men struggling towards anything that would float. He leaped into the water, and as he sank into the depths he felt his boots striking something. Fighting his way to the surface he emerged to find he was staring into the face of Elliot, another ex-boy that he knew well! They spluttered a greeting while Elliot exclaimed, "Some bastard with big boots jumped right on my head!" "What a shit," said Hutchison.

Within a short time, all sorts of craft were picking up the struggling swimmers. One of the French fishing boats took a load of survivors, including Hutchison, to Devonport, Plymouth, where on the quayside they were given cups of tea by wives from the naval married quarters. The women were astonished to find one survivor clad only in a blanket, and several of the wives went home and returned with a suit, shirt, socks and shoes, and even a trilby hat, having raided their absent husbands' wardrobes.

Hutchison and many others returned after the war to visit the graves where the friendly Bretons had buried hundreds of drowned servicemen whom they had recovered from the sea. Thinking over these and many other incidents, I came to recognize that I had been astonishingly fortunate in escaping injury and capture during the evacuation of France, especially as the Dunkirk area became increasingly hazardous in the remaining days after I had departed in HMS Esk.

The Dunkirk evacuation took place between May 27 and June 4, 1940. It would be exactly four years before a much better trained and equipped British Army set foot in France.

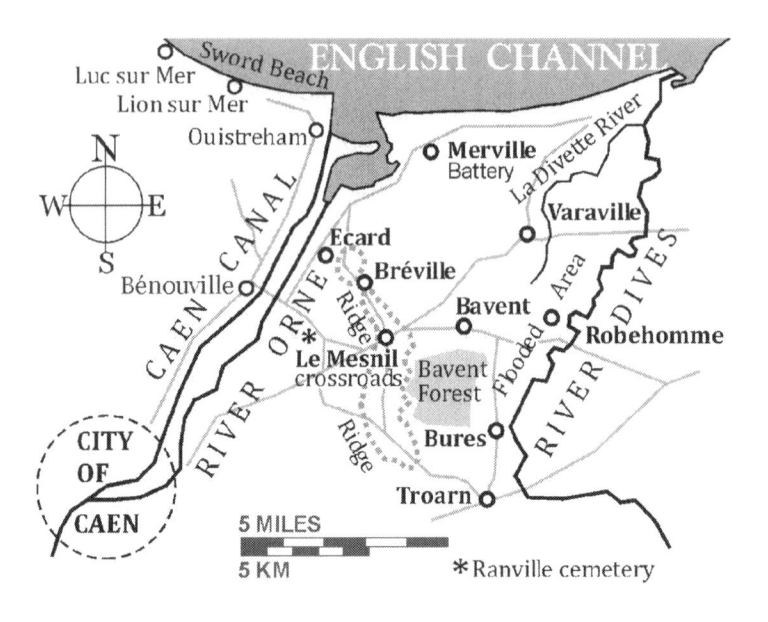

6th Airborne Division Combat Area
Normandy, France, June-August 1944

D-Day: Into Action by Air

As my head cleared I was conscious of the wet grass pressing up against my face. I could feel a raw stinging around my ears and my hands came away wet. Through a searing headache I could hear machine gun fire, and as I struggled to my knees I suddenly realized - I was in France. Then I remembered ... I was in the 6th Airborne Division, 3rd Parachute Squadron RE (the Royal Engineer component of the 3rd Parachute Brigade) and this was Operation Tonga, the airborne section of Operation Overlord (the overall Allied invasion of Normandy). Dropped by parachute just east of the city of Caen, the major objectives of the 6th Airborne included capturing intact the critical pair of bridges over the Caen canal and the Orne river; holding that area against enemy counter-attacks while awaiting reinforcements; and destroying a series of bridges across the River Dives to stop any German forces coming from the east to help repel the sea-borne Allied invasion at the western Normandy beaches - Operation Neptune.

Failure to capture the Bénouville bridge (over the canal) and the Ranville bridge (over the river) would also have left our 6th Division cut off from essential supplies and reinforcements due in from British ground forces arriving at Sword Beach on the nearest section of Normandy's west coast. The night raid to secure them had fallen to a very fit 'D' Company, 2nd Battalion (Airborne). Six Horsa gliders (three for each bridge) carrying platoons of infantry and five sappers per plane were flown in with amazing accuracy (except one) and landed within a few hundred feet of their targets. The infantry were to overcome the German troops on guard while the engineers located and defused any demolition explosives. For six days and nights these men had practised their mission just outside Exeter in southwest England, where two very similar bridges spanned the river Exe.

The bridges were taken just after midnight, the canal bridge at Bénouville first, the infantry from the leading gliders dispatching the surprised enemy with grenades and machine guns. Minutes later the river bridge was captured with small arms and mortar fire. These firefights also incurred the first Allied deaths of the Normandy invasion, including No.1 glider's platoon commander. When German armour approached the canal bridge from Bénouville, the leading tank was blown up by a crucial shot from 'D' Company's sole PIAT anti-tank weapon. Its fiery destruction caused the following tanks to withdraw, buying precious time.

The first reinforcements from 7th Parachute Battalion soon arrived and set up positions in Bénouville. German forces there mobilized and attacked them with mortar fire and machine guns throughout the night, but could not break the British line and so waited for tank support. In the morning, two German gunboats approaching from Ouistreham were driven back from the canal bridge. A solitary German aircraft managed to hit the canal bridge with one bomb - but it failed to explode! Thirteen of the next seventeen German tanks sent to retake the bridges were destroyed by the 7th Parachute Battalion (despite their being undermanned) with PIATs and Gammon bombs.

'D' company platoons then cleared out the Germans around Bénouville in house-to-house fighting. Shortly after midday the 1st Commando Brigade that had landed at Sword Beach arrived, and some Allied tanks. A boatload of German infantry approaching from Caen was promptly shelled into retreat. That evening 2nd Battalion infantry arrived from Sword Beach and took up defensive positions. For a week they held the bridges by various means, including the use of intense anti-aircraft fire against German bombers.

On June 14th (my 24th birthday!) the 51st Infantry Division moved in to take over the task from 6th Airborne, and they were soon joined by Dutch and Belgian troops. The Bénouville bridge over the Caen canal was renamed Pegasus bridge (and remains so to this day, in honour of the 6th Airborne). Ranville bridge over the Orne river was renamed Horsa bridge. The initial operation (called Operation Deadstick) of capturing and holding those two objectives took place a few miles west of where I was about to land on D-Day, and was vital to the success of our own missions.

Monday 5th June 1944. We took off in Douglas Dakota No. 249. There were hundreds of paratrooper planes and Horsa gliders in the sky, and there was still enough dusk light to see them. The sky slowly darkened as we circled around, gradually coming into echelon (formation), before we headed south. Sixteen men were in my plane. Captain Smith was number one. Every man, including myself, was jittery and excited but trying not to show it. Our faces were daubed nearly black.

I had a felt-cloth valise (travel bag) containing a Sten gun and magazine strapped to my right leg, with a haversack and respirator secured on the outside. The valise was fixed so that when a pin was pulled the bag was released and could be lowered to the twenty-foot extent of its cord. This allowed it to hit the ground before the parachutist, his descent thereby being slowed just before landing. Also packed around me and in various pouches and pockets were a fighting knife, 2 Mills bombs, a smoke grenade, a Gammon bomb (bag with draw-string and detonator attached), 2 pounds of PHE (plastic high explosive), 7 full Sten gun magazines, 50 rounds of 303" ammo, an entrenching tool, detonators, maps, binoculars, compass, watch, jack knife - and my escape kit.

The escape kit included a 3-inch piece of hacksaw blade covered in waxed paper and hidden in the seam of a breast pocket of my serge blouse, a map of France printed on silk in a trouser pocket, and a phrase book written in several languages. My inner smock had sleeves, large pockets, plus a crotch piece secured by large press-studs, and my equipment was worn over the smock. A zipped-up sleeveless jumping smock then covered all the worn equipment from thighs to neck. Wound around me was a toggle rope six feet long, having a loop spliced into one end and a toggle at the other. One of my trouser buttons looked like brass, just like the rest, but was in fact magnetised steel, and if placed on a flat surface it would turn until a slight indentation on the button faced north - a secret compass.

My khaki trousers had large patch pockets on the thighs and two seat pockets containing two large field dressings, which would help cushion spine impact during a poor landing. Also in my kit was a small syringe of morphine, the one-inch needle being protected by a plastic cap. On my left wrist was a watch, and on the right wrist a compass. On my feet were standard ammunition boots with gaiters over the ankles. Four straps, two behind the ears and two in front, secured my steel helmet, the straps being joined to a snugly fitted chin-pad. The last item to be added, before I zipped myself up, was a torch (flashlight) so that I could easily get at it by opening the zip a little. Over the jumping smock was my parachute, the harness terminating in a robust box on my chest from which the straps could be released.

Then there was a life jacket (a rubber tube secured by tapes) which could be inflated by mouth. From the back of the parachute emerged a static line, this being a long woven strap folded on itself and held in position by neat shock cords. The outer end was secured to a steel cable running along the roof of the plane. When I jumped, the static line would be extended and would pull out my chute as I was falling, and a final tie string would then break, allowing the chute to open. Each of the rest of the 'stick' of sixteen men was similarly equipped, unless he carried a different weapon such as a Bren gun or a two-inch mortar. Being number eight, I would be in the middle when we left the plane, and I was to shine the torch as we were descending, giving the others a direction to head for when reaching the ground. My torch had a blue filter. The eighth men in other planes had different coloured filters, to reduce confusion with other units while trying to keep their own together.

We passed tea around as we crossed the English coast, before the lights were shut off. We managed to sing:
*"There was Brown, upside down,
mopping up the whisky on the floor ..."*
But the singing was a bit croaky, and soon the chatter died away. The plane was steady over the English Channel but we could see nothing on the water. We couldn't even see our static lines. The door was on the port side, and sitting next to it was Captain Smith. I was on starboard side, and there were three men to my left, numbers six, four and two - number two being opposite the door. Our seats were plain fore-and-aft benches fixed against the sides of the plane. We saw flashes over the French coast on our right front. These were from 4,000 lb bombs being dropped by 100 Lancasters on a German ack-ack site. We all stood up as we crossed the French coast and the red light went on.

Suddenly there were flashes in the sky all around us. The plane pitched and shook from AA (anti-aircraft) fire, and the noise was deafening. Then a big lurch just as the green light went on threw everybody down, some on their knees, all mixed up with static lines in the dark. We got up, scrambled towards the door and jumped out as fast as we could, but it was pitch dark with just the shape of the door to guide us. I went out like a crab and got kicked around in the slipstream. My helmet came off and took some skin from the backs of my ears with it. I was soon trying to wave the blue light and loosen my valise with the Sten at the same time. Some red spots appeared in front of me, quickly widening and growing large as they drew near and then shot past me into the sky. Someone was firing at me - he could see my torch. I instinctively dropped it, and watched it blinking alternately as it rotated and grew smaller far below me. The Sten and my haversack had fallen like a stone and broken the cord, and that was the last I saw of them. Plenty of AA fire continued, tracers and so on. Then I saw the ground, half of it a confusing mirror of water, and I was about to figure this out when it rushed up towards me and I frantically tried to prepare for the tumble.

It must have been about 0130 hours when I hit the earth, but I have no recollection of it. I regained consciousness at about three in the morning, in cold wet grass. And this was when, through my splitting head pain, the realisation that I was in France swept over me. Somebody had removed my harness, life belt, jumping jacket and other accessories. There was still AA fire and plenty of machine guns bursting. I saw only one man near me. I whispered, "Who's that?" "Joe!" It was Joe Hewitt, the 'jester' of my stick. Why he waited there with me I never found out.

Back when our squadron had been assembled and briefed in the transit camp in Wiltshire (June 3rd at RAF Blakehill Farm) we had been told to go southwest from our para-drop, so Joe and I did this by compass, ignoring the fact that we should have been on higher ground looking for an RV (rendezvous) light in a fold in the ground. We went onward for about two hours, but there was nothing but shallow water, with one ditch about six-foot deep, which we soon discovered when we fell into it. I had no weapon, so I primed a Mills bomb, that is, I inserted a detonator and fuse but left the pin in position. And I kept the knife handy, not that I had much hope. If a Jerry saw us splashing across that water, he would have just waited until we were near and then let us have it. After the first wetting we joined our toggle ropes and took turns walking in front, thinking that was the way for only one of us to get wet, and then the other could pull him out. We had various schemes for crossing a really wide ditch, but fortunately never encountered anything so big.

As it got lighter, we saw a farmhouse on rising ground, and by then we had been soaked a few times and the going was hard. We crept up very close, seeing parachutes lying in the bushes, and one up in a tree. A man came out and I called softly, "M'sieur, nous sommes Anglais. Où sont les Boschs?" He froze for a moment, then came towards us and shook hands. He said there were plenty of Germans in Bavent, but we were on the east side of Robehomme and there were none here. "Attendez!" he said and went into the house, then reappeared with a bottle. "Hey, Joe, it's cider," I said, and took a swig. But it was Calvados apple brandy - just what we needed - and right then his wife and children came out to shake hands too. We said thank you and walked towards the village. We could hear firing, but it was miles away. There were only a few houses, but people kept appearing, and everyone was eager to shake hands, especially the older folks. One man gave us a 'poor' sandwich, all fat and brown bread - bless him - and told us our men were eastwards. We went to the east for a quarter mile when a boy stopped us and said he had seen "Les Berets Rouge", and soon we met some 9th Parachute Battalion chaps, just three of them.

The primary D-Day task assigned to the 9th was the silencing of the Merville Gun Battery, where the Germans were in a position to threaten the British landings on the nearby coast. Due to a disastrous parachute drop, only one quarter of their force managed to assemble and attack the battery, while the rest were scattered over a wide area, like so many of the division. While talking with these fellows about our respective locations, a Jeep and trailer overloaded with men from our own 3rd Troop went past at a nearby road junction. So we hailed them, and joined their mission to one of our own objectives, a bridge over the River Dives, east of Robehomme, where we helped in demolishing the abutments.

We discovered that about seventy men were in this area. Sergeant Poole had para-dropped here with a crowd of Canadians from their 1st Parachute Batallion. He had recognized the Robehomme bridge from the models used for the briefing at RAF Blakehill Farm. When the expected backup RE's with the planned explosives had failed to arrive on time, Sergeant Poole had collected two pounds each of PHE from a number of the Canadians until he had about 30 pounds, enough to single-handedly demolish the bridge. He had cut it in the centre, and each half had fallen into the river. When the other RE sappers finally did arrive with more explosives, they set to using 'beehives' and PHE to demolish the concrete abutments, with the aim of making it very difficult for the enemy to rebuild any form of bridge.

PHE, being plastic high explosive, is not easy to use for this work because it comes in eight-ounce sticks that are eight inches long and wrapped in waxed paper. So a hole is first made in the concrete using a beehive, which is a six-pound charge shaped around a hollow bronze cone standing on three legs. When detonated, the explosive instantly drives the cone down between the three legs as a fig-sized lump of nearly molten metal, which will penetrate about three feet of concrete. A second beehive might increase the depth by six or eight inches. Then a rod with a spoon shaped end is used to fish out the hot metal, or else the subsequently loaded explosive may ignite or even detonate while it is being primed. The paper on the PHE is slit open so that when they are pressed the plastic sticks can be shaped like putty to fill the irregularly shaped hole. A fiddly job to be sure, and not as neat as a drilled hole, but a quick and effective method.

Meantime some German truck troops passed the crossroads less than half a mile to the east. There were some Canadian boys on the far bank giving us protection, so I grabbed some PHE and strapped it to one of the tall poplars on the bank. I used a detonator and safety fuse, and called a warning. About four pounds went off with one hell of a bang, but it didn't cut right through the tree, which stayed up for nearly a minute with its branches entwined in its neighbours. Then it fell exactly the way I had wanted across the river. Its branches were nearly submerged on the far side, and it was a pretty makeshift bridge, but I expect the Canadians found it better than nothing. Certainly better than swimming for it with those Germans coming up behind them! And there was still enough time to set a second charge in the middle of the tree and blow it in half, so that the pieces floated apart and the enemy could not use that way of crossing the water.

In another couple of minutes we were under fire. The enemy had a gun too, which we had seen as they zipped over the crossroads, and they soon got the range and lobbed a few right on the abutments. By then I had sprinted to a roadside ditch and jumped in to find Jack Doyle there too. We had been boy-soldiers together, but this was hardly the time to chat! Amongst the racket of small shells and small arms fire, we could hear a Schmeisser submachine gun very loud and fast, and then I saw an abandoned haversack and a fighting knife right there under my nose. As I grabbed these I felt an insistent tapping on my left leg. I turned to see who it was, and saw that there were bits of concrete coming from an overhead power line pole near my left leg, the chips flying from a point a foot above my head. I was out of there in a flash, backwards along the ditch, feet first and face down. The Schmeisser gunner had obviously had me in his sights, but maybe he had set them too high. When I finally made a run for it, I found out that Sergeant Poole had arranged covering fire, which also enabled two Bren Gunners, Spike and Taffy, to withdraw. The enemy pulled back shortly after we did.

In the area of Robehomme village, where we were grouped, we were well clear of the enemy, and also on higher ground, so we dug slit trenches for ourselves. I was exhausted but lit a small fire using dry wild parsnip roots, and pulled out a piece of dehydrated mutton from the 24-hour ration packs in my newly acquired haversack. The mutton was nearly white with flecks of grey - mostly fat with a little lean. It was two inches square by an inch thick, and I added water and heated it in the mess tin. I've had better, but I ate it with Horlicks flavoured biscuits, and drank some tea made from cubes of compressed dried milk mixed with tea leaves. I finished with a boiled sweet and a cigarette as I lay in my slit trench, still a bit wet but reasonably comfortable in the warm sunshine.

In the evening I found myself a Sten gun, a few being available from the wounded chaps. No one had been hurt at the bridge, so I guessed that their injuries were from difficult parachute landings. I couldn't control my speech very well, and during the night I was quite cold, shivering a lot, probably from a slight concussion. It appeared that we were isolated: no contact with the troops to the west at Le Mesnil, and with the enemy occupying Bavent between Le Mesnil and ourselves. Next morning we were detailed off for various jobs by Lance Sergeant Wren. I was sent with another sapper to crater (blow a hole in) a minor road to the north. We were driven there in a Jeep, with four packs of explosive and beehives. Although the road looked more like a cart track through swampy ground, the beehives kept punching through well-compacted rubble. The last beehive went off and a bit of flying metal punctured a pack I had carelessly left by the roadside about twenty feet away. We heard and saw the explosive in the pack burning like a blowlamp, so we kept our heads down until it all fizzled out.

Fishing out the hot lumps of metal from the cavity made by the beehives took some time, but finally the crater we produced with plastic explosives packed into that hole would have at least stopped a truck. Even a tank might have had some difficulty trying to bypass it, considering the swampy ground bordering the road. We did a good job with the tools available, I said to myself as we made our way back.

The main group was making preparations for a move during the coming night. A horse and cart had been commandeered to transport the wounded, and a group of Canadians were busy wrapping the steel wheel treads with rags to deaden the noise. The jeep and trailer were still nearly full of explosives. We were told that whereas Le Mesnil (where our 3rd Troop was centred) was about four miles west of us, we would initially go south, then west, then north, mostly in the forest, the Bois de Bavent, to avoid Bavent itself, which was in enemy hands. A point section would go first to check for opposition, and then the main party would follow.

After dusk fell we were on our way, departing the dark shuttered houses where not a sign of life was evident. There was sporadic firing from various directions, and since I was the first man in the main party I was wondering who we might bump into next. After a while we were shifted around and someone else took the lead. We came upon a German pickup slewed into the roadside, with bodies in it and also on the road. Our point section had ambushed them. I was assigned to check if anyone was still alive, and I instructed Sapper Benson to help me. I found that the stench of freshly killed humans, maybe a dozen of them, was quite shattering. Benny, prodding bodies with a bayonet, suddenly gave out a cry of surprise and a strangled whisper, "He's alive!" Actually it was simply the dead man's innards making noises while being poked. Meanwhile we were hearing groans and faint splashes from a wounded German who had escaped in a flooded area to our left, but we couldn't spend time searching a waterlogged place in the dark. We pressed on, and after an hour or so met a patrol in the dark woods where a few egg bombs were lobbed at us. Egg bombs were noisy but with negligible shrapnel, and we soon scared the enemy away with grenades. Things then got a bit boring. It seemed the advance section was having trouble ensuring we were on the right track, so we had several waits and actually dropped off to sleep until awoken by an extremely irate fellow who had come back to look for us. Dawn was breaking as we pushed through thick undergrowth where an armoured car was covered with scrim netting. Then we were on the road just a short distance from Le Mesnil crossroads.

Sergeant Docherty shepherded the sappers into positions along a hedgerow running east from the crossroads, directing Sapper Glover and me to a vacant slit trench. Two 9th Parachute Battalion boys had dug it, and they were lying dead a few feet away, looking very peaceful, with only several tiny shrapnel holes in their airborne smocks to indicate how they had died. In front of us was the road to Bavent, only a matter of feet away, but the slit trenches were well hidden amongst brambles and small trees in the hedgerow. The ground fell away on the far side of the road, to rough pasture and then trees, so an approaching enemy would be seen while we were still hidden. In the fifth or sixth slit trench to the right was Lieutenant Holloway, a most likeable officer with an admirable spread of moustache. He shared the trench with a Bren gunner. The field behind us was full of apple trees, and there were more bodies piled under the nearest one. Within an hour we heard the unmistakeable noise of heavy mortars to our front and right front, and then the bombs were falling among our positions.

This was to continue - mortars at first light or soon after - and then several times during the day. Sometimes the mortar bombs were followed immediately by Schmeisser and Spandau machine gun fire, as well as sniper fire. We could hear Germans shouting orders, and they weren't far away, but very difficult to see since they kept well hidden in the thick undergrowth. We would get odd glimpses of grey uniforms and would fire at where they ought to be. After an attack, stretcher-bearers would sometimes be trotting along just behind us in the orchard, going empty and returning with a wounded man. On occasions the man was dead and the corpse was tipped on the pile. After a couple of days all the corpses were removed, to be buried I assumed, and I didn't much care to think about how that was organized.

I admired those stretcher-bearers. I found out afterwards that at least two of them were non-combatants.

I didn't keep a diary at this time, and failed to note the proper sequence of events, but during the first few days we had hot food delivered to us, both nourishment and words of cheer coming from Sergeant Docherty on most occasions. He brought the food from some place west of us, where a hundred yards away there was a brickyard (in Le Mesnil) and where the 9th Parachute Battalion boys had set up their three-inch mortars. Meanwhile, Lieutenant Holloway was making a determined effort to drive out some snipers from a farm building within his view but not mine. He asked me for covering fire and I gave it, spraying short bursts into any likely looking spots in the bushes and trees fifty or more yards to my front. He called out that he didn't want that, so I desisted and watched my front intently while he got into position quickly and started firing along the road with a Bren. His targets were a farm outhouse on the left of the road and the farm on the right. Single individuals sprinted across at rare intervals, their aim being to man machine guns in the outhouse. It is likely that he winged a few because their activity ceased.

But the main activity in those first few days was the mortaring, which was reinforced sometimes by rocket-propelled bombs that were truly horrific. The ordinary mortars were bad enough, with their awful thumps preceding the screeching descents. And then the whanging cracks as they exploded, spreading injury and death to anyone unlucky enough to be nearby. The rockets, however, were far louder than ordinary mortars, and when first fired emitted screaming animal-like groans which made one's skin crawl, soon followed by an increasing irregular whistling as they approached, and finally deafening crashes as the salvo exploded. I saw a partially exploded rocket-bomb that looked as if one end of a four-foot steel gas bottle had been split into five or six strips peeled back like a banana skin. Usually the whole thing disintegrated into flying shrapnel, which could be heard continuing to whine after the main explosion. These were the infamous rocket-launched Nebelwerfers (smoke mortars) that had been developed by the Wehrmacht's so-called Nebeltruppen (smoke troops). The bombs were given their name as a disinformation strategy designed to fool observers into thinking that they were merely smoke screens, when in fact they delivered a more powerful explosive than any artillery shell of the same weight.

During one period there were lots of pamphlets scattered about, lying in the hedgerows and fields and reputed to have arrived by rocket. They told us that the Americans in England were seducing our women, that we were pawns in a losing game and were certainly going to get killed if we continued fighting, and that we would be well treated if we surrendered right away. The messages were completely ignored.

Most often mortars and rockets would start at first light, and then salvos at odd times during the day. Sometimes a mortar attack would be followed immediately by machine gun fire, but of course machine gun fire alone might happen at any time. On one occasion I scraped a hole with my entrenching tool, fifteen feet from the trench. I dropped my trousers to answer the call of nature when machine guns started up and cut some twigs and brambles near me. I finished my business flat on my back, concentrating on a quick and tidy return to the trench. It was one of the few occasions when Glover and I had a really good laugh, which was a bit squeaky but did us a world of good. We got snippets of news as time went on, some good, some bad, names of casualties and worse, like the report that Lance Corporal Gillette had been killed by mortar fire. I had known Razorblades (his nickname of course) very well indeed, and he had often said that he would get it, something that I could not understand. I always figured that one had to have hope.

During the first few days, three Canadians came quickly along the hedgerow, glancing around in all directions. The 1st Canadian Parachute Battalion had been incorporated into the British 3rd Parachute Brigade for D-Day. Among their assigned tasks were to support the 9th Parachute Battalion and to protect 3rd Parachute Squadron engineers while they prepared to blow up bridges, lay minefields and so on. "Seen any Heinies?" one said, carrying a Bren across his middle with the sling over his shoulder. The second had a sniper's rifle with a telescopic sight, and the third had a two-inch mortar and a rack with a few bombs. They were carrying a tidy weight between them, and they kept trotting on - hunting!

Brave men. I wasn't brave in those first few days. I didn't sleep. My body felt like lead, and it was an effort to move. But I got to know myself better. I had long ago come to the assumption that if there was a Supreme Being it probably wasn't anything like the god portrayed in the writings in the Bible, but during a particularly low period I was really terrified, during a vicious hammering by mortars. The incessant blasting, with associated shouts from the enemy and screams from some wounded men, resulted in my saying prayers with frantic urgency but - and this is the strange part - I really wasn't sure that any one was listening. For the rest of the day I thought hard about it.

I knew that it was ingrained in me to pray - it had been pounded into my head as a child in Sunday school and at day school prayers. But on this occasion I had been terrified out of my wits. I had been scared many times before, particularly during events leading up to Dunkirk, and at Dunkirk, but not like this. I decided that from now on, whenever I was frightened, I would not mumble prayers. And so I got better (if that is the term) as the days passed, and cheered up somewhat. On the second day I was heartily cheered. Looking to my left I saw Brigadier Hill, the recipient of many medals for bravery and commander of our 3rd Parachute Brigade, carrying his signature walking stick! He was followed by a sergeant of the APTS (Army Physical Training Staff) carrying a slung Bren. "Good morning," said the brigadier brightly and with a slight smile. He was limping a little, having been wounded in the tail-end during the parachute jump.

Most of the time we were making a conscious effort to put scary thoughts behind us and act normally. We chatted a lot about all sorts of things, *anything* to push behind us the terrible events that happened every day. We used an interesting password system. Instead of the usual, "Halt! Who goes there?" the challenger might say, "Punch," and the one challenged would reply, "and Judy," this being the arrangement for that day. One day it was, "King," to which one had to reply, "and Country." One paratrooper heard someone approaching in the darkness and called out, "King!" The person approaching stood still and said nothing. He was challenged again, still without reply, so the challenger shot him dead. Shortly afterward we found out that he was one of our own. For the next couple of days the challenger wept, in between phases of hysteria and near violence. He was then returned to England, and we never heard the outcome. Lots of theories were discussed, and it was generally accepted that his victim had frozen in fright, becoming tongue-tied during those crucial seconds, and that the hapless shooter, overcome with constant remorse, subsequently suffered a nervous breakdown.

Our briefing in the transit camp at RAF Blakehill Farm in Wiltshire was also discussed at length. All agreed that it had been outstanding. The models were mostly made of canvas and paint. Bits of shredded sponge plastic skewered on pieces of wood served as trees. Whole areas were exhibited on tables inside large marquees: replicas complete with hills, woods, streams, gardens, and houses - the lot! After the first lectures we were free to visit the mock-ups at any time, and to see the photographs on display. The bridges scheduled for demolition were of particular interest. They had been photographed by low flying aircraft, and the pictures carefully enlarged. The steel members were dimensioned with surprising accuracy.

It was during this stay at the camp near Le Mesnil that the whole division was addressed by General Gale, an impressive figure in riding breeches with gleaming boots topped by an airborne smock! Gale (nicknamed 'Windy') had been instrumental in persuading his military superiors (including Major-General Browning and also those above him) that the entire 6th Division would be required to successfully pull off Operation Tonga, not just a smaller group from the 6th as initially planned. General Gale's speech was the only occasion I can remember where we were ordered to "Sit to attention!" Several men had automatically started to rise when they heard the order, "Attention!"

The 1st Canadian Parachute Battalion had a large percentage of North American Indians among them. Real Red Indians! I remember seven of them posing with heads bent for a picture. Each head was shaved with enough hair remaining to spell out a single letter, and together they spelled, "VICTORY".

There was a canteen in the camp, but I don't remember having much to drink. Well, maybe one pint! We did all sorts of things to pass the time. I made quite an elaborate valise out of half-inch thick felt, which along with its gaiter was to be attached to my leg.

Within the perimeter fence there was a farm, so I suppose the farming family were incarcerated until we left. I remember Bill Irving helping the farmer butcher a pig. Two double apron barbed wire fences surrounded our camp, and those on guard duty - our own men - were ordered to shoot anyone found between the double aprons. This was a measure of the precautions taken to ensure that only those authorized were to have any contact with anyone outside.

On our final night in camp we had a concert. An outstanding item was when three brigadiers, including our Brigadier Hill, sang:
Mares eat oats, and does eat oats, and little lambs eat ivy,
Doodely Doody Doo, Doody Doo...
This light relief was greeted with an enthusiastic roar.

I now realized that we were filling a gap in an infantry position until the units got themselves sorted out. My unit, the 3rd Parachute Squadron RE, was to carry out sapper duties when required, but in the meantime we helped by filling out the perimeter. In our days of briefing before D-Day take-off (and now highlighted by the address given by General Gale) we had had plenty of time to get to know our objectives. Our Division, the 6th Airborne, was to occupy the eastern bridgehead. Our 'patch' was a piece of France stretching from the sea to about eight miles inland, bounded on the west by the River Orne and the Caen Canal (which was parallel and close to the river) and on the east by the River Dives about five miles away.

Among the many engineering jobs, including clearing anti-glider obstacles and demolishing a coastal battery, our Squadron had the tasks of destroying bridges in the Dives valley: at Varaville nearest the sea, Robehomme, Bures and at Troarn. The troop I was with had been assigned the Robehomme bridge, this being where I had helped with beehives and road cratering. Also at that time our squadron commander, Major Roseveare ('Rosie') had taken a jeep and trailer loaded with men and explosives through some wicked small-arms fire to the Troarn bridge and cut right through its main arch. Captain Juckes had led a troop that had blown up two bridges at Bures, and then did more damage to the remaining masonry at the Troarn bridge site. Part of my troop had demolished the Varaville bridge.

Considering that the Dives valley was flooded, and with an enemy active throughout the area, and that ack-ack action had forced the planes carrying parachutists and the planes towing Horsa gliders to miss their targets by many miles in some cases, the fact that these Dives bridges were destroyed was not only praiseworthy, it was incredible. It would now be very difficult for the enemy to gain access to us from east of the Dives valley because any bridge equipment would require transport by road, and the Allies had air supremacy.

Now the Division was dug in on the high ridge of ground between the Orne and the Dives, not in a continuous line or area, but in pockets. The whole area was held and patrolled by both Germans and Allies, and it was common for our patrols to go one way safely but to run into the enemy when trying to return by another route, and vice versa. By this time we were quite used to seeing numbers of German prisoners, usually marching under escort back to the pens. It was well known that our German-speaking Canadians were 'grilling' some of them. The Le Mesnil area, where I happened to be dug in, had become the headquarters of the 3rd Parachute Brigade, of which the 3rd Parachute Squadron RE was a part. A field ambulance unit was there too, and they were all located within a couple of hundred yards of me, in the trees and across the road from the brickyard.

On several occasions a jeep passed in front of us, collecting wounded. A medic sat beside the stretcher, and there was a bottle of plasma on a fixture above the stretcher, sometimes connected to a wounded man. I really did admire them. They made a sizeable target for the enemy during their mercy trips. Then there was a time when I saw a wounded man lying unconscious in a hedgerow, but when I called a medic he said he knew about him, that he was a hopeless case due to terrible wounds, and they were leaving him to die quietly. I was very subdued for some time.

The brickyard owner, a Monsieur DuPont, was still occupying his house in the brickyard, as were the three-inch mortar sections of some parachute battalions. I was directed to take some corrugated iron sheeting, which I needed for a job, from the brickyard. This resulted in voluble protests from Monsieur DuPont, who claimed he needed the sheets for a shelter for his family. He was overruled by an officer, so I received my corrugated sheets. Only a mile or so to the northwest of Le Mesnil the tiny town of Bréville was occupied by the enemy, who were not driven out until the night of 12th June after many murderous encounters. Two hundred German dead were counted there.

We were moved about during some phases of these Bréville battles, and on one such move were digging in on a patch where the ground was very rocky, so we were not making much progress, in spite of encouragement by our commander, Rosie Roseveare. He kept saying, "Dig or die!" which made us wonder what was coming at us next. But the battle did not come that close on that occasion, although I remember seeing one chap, wounded by mortar fragments and trying hard to look unconcerned as two colleagues helped him back, white faced and unsteady on his feet.

Shortly after the Bréville area had been cleared, I was occupying a slit trench, which I had dug with Spike the Bren gunner, right opposite the brickworks. There were others there in trenches already, and more came to join us, forming an engineering pool that could, and did, supply sappers for various duties. General Gale, as Divisional Commander, was 'holding court' with some others about twenty yards from our trench one day, and I found it interesting to observe them. I couldn't hear it well enough, but I could see the general talking, and fifteen or so officers paying close attention. Then the enemy started mortaring, the bombs falling a little too close for comfort, and some officers were looking around uncomfortably. But the general continued to talk, with sublime unconcern. I thought there was something quite admirable about his presence, but I would really like to have known just what he was thinking. After all, no man, unless he is an idiot, is completely without fear.

I wasn't too happy myself, thinking that if a bomb should hit the high branches near me we would be the recipients of shrapnel from a very dangerous angle. By this time I had got myself a rifle, which made me feel a lot better because I had a very low opinion of a Sten gun. For anything over fifty yards I considered it about as much use as a catapult, having carried out many experiments with a Sten on a miniature range.

We heard that Rosie Roseveare had promoted a sapper called Banbury to lance corporal. On his many visits to HQ and to other units, Rosie took Banbury with him, arming Banbury with a Bren gun, emulating Brigadier Hill with his bodyguard. Banbury could not drive, whereas Rosie drove like a bat. I suppose having a bodyguard added prestige, and it was useful to have the jeep watched while at a meeting. The arrangement did not work so well, because Banbury used to get bored while waiting and would soon skedaddle to the nearest estaminet, so Rosie would have to find him and drag him out. On one such occasion Banbury was still arguing while Rosie whipped the jeep up to speed. Banbury decided he wanted to go back and leaped out, breaking both legs. He was shipped out to England and eventually returned to us. Before being interviewed by Rosie, Banbury took off his lance corporal stripes. "Aha! I see you've saved me the trouble," observed Rosie.

It was decided to mine the road to Bavent, right in front of my old slit trench. An officer and I laid the mines within an area marked by a single strand of barbed wire carrying warning notices. We covered each anti-tank mine with an inch or so of material, matching the fill to the surrounding road surface. He was booking it all (recording it) and after laying one area I walked off to get something across the road. I then froze, realizing what I had done. I was standing in the middle of the minefield, surrounded by well-concealed mines. He was marvellous, talking quietly to me while he studied his records. Then he told me what to do, "Turn left, take two paces forward ... and now turn right, take three paces forward," and so on until I reached the perimeter wire safely. Then we both pushed on with the job. He didn't mention it again, to me or to anyone else. What a gent!

Shortly after this (around June 15th), the 3rd Para Sqdn RE moved to a disused quarry at a hamlet called Ecarde (La Haute Ecarde), down the ridge and westwards towards the Orne River. It felt safer, and it was, in so far as mortar fire went. But we kept doing the same sort of work amongst the dug-in paratroop boys. Spike and I dug another trench, and next to it I made a tent out of khaki parachute silk, erected on a grassy mound. It was very comfortable to sit in during an off duty period - except the occasion when there was a loud crack and a bullet hole in the silk on either side of me. What the...? I dashed outside, and there was Spike with his Bren gun, looking very shame-faced. He had let one off 'up the spout' while cleaning his gun. We didn't speak for a while. Well, there wasn't much he could say was there?

Soldiers did some strange things - like me in the minefield for example. And a junior NCO like myself had a thankless and awkward task. He was always with the men, eating, washing, showering and sleeping, with no privacy, supposedly a superior, but when orders were passed down he was on the receiving end and had to deal directly with the men who carried them out, often alongside and helping them. I got on well with Spike, and he appreciated all this and never embarrassed me, never took advantage of our friendship, so I wasn't going to let a little thing like a bullet whizzing past my ear unduly upset me.

At about this time it was quietly passed around that if a man thought his part in an action was worthy of mention, he should write a report of it and get a couple of witnesses to agree to the account. I could not imagine myself doing such a thing, and looked upon the idea as touting for medals. Not for me! But it gave me much to think about. I have often since wondered if a particular decoration was awarded because of the recipient's colourful description of outstanding or perilous action rather than what really took place.

But we did have some rousing stories to share, and many with sad endings. During the para-drop on D-Day, a number of the lost ones or misplaced arrivals had their own tales to tell. Some became closely engaged with the enemy right away, and in the confusion there were quite a few sappers captured who subsequently escaped. Captain Jack was interned immediately on touching down right inside the enemy's Anti-para Kommando HQ, but got away in the early morning and arrived at Le Mesnil by 9am! Some individuals were involved in remarkably offensive action against the Germans. Sapper Thomas was shot as he was coming down, but killed 3 Germans with his grenades. The late Sergeant Jones was taken and somehow turned the tables to get the upper hand, killing eight of his captors using their own weapons! Squadron QM Sergeant Brown was injured on the drop and still managed to kill a large number of Germans with his Sten. The only officer of whom there had been no further trace after the drop was Lieutenant Knox, who was known to have been shot during his descent but had been seen alive on landing.

When Major Roseveare had arrived in Troarn shortly before 5am on D-Day, to demolish its bridge just east of the town, his jeep and trailer carried a load of some 3,000 pounds (including Lieutenant Breese, seven NCO sappers and the explosives) and could only go at a speed of 35 mph. As they passed through the town, Germans fired at them from practically every doorway. Fortunately the main street sloped downhill and provided a rapid getaway. During this firefight, Major Roseveare reported that his Bren gunner, sapper Peachey, had done a magnificent rearguard job through town. But when the jeep and its heavy trailer, which had careened from side to side due to the increased speed, finally reached the bridge, sapper Peachey and his Bren were both missing. The good news was that the bridge itself was not under enemy guard. After the demolition of the central span, Major Roseveare's party withdrew northward before being forced to ditch the transport. And then they swam through several streams and hiked via the Bavent Forest to reach Le Mesnil, arriving there shortly after noon.

Captain Juckes had also set an inspiring example in the early hours of June 6th at the two bridges that were demolished at Bures. His group of 3rd Squadron RE included Lieutenants Shave, Wade and Lack, and Sergeant Shrubsole. They had not received any news of Major Roseveare's successful mission, so after a brief rest and meal at Bures his group continued south to Troarn and through another small arms firefight down the main street, during which they took many prisoners. Finding the damage that was already done, they proceeded to blow up a second section of the bridge, while cheerful local French townsfolk furnished them with wine and food. After this they withdrew to rejoin the 8th Battalion in the Bavent Forest and from there made their way to 3rd Para Brigade HQ at Le Mesnil.

It was at Le Mesnil that our well-liked and admired Captain Juckes was later killed, aged 24, sitting in his parked jeep. He was about to report on the sappers placement of sandbags around the 1st Canadian Para area, when a mortar bomb that no one heard coming exploded just two yards away, mortally wounding him but amazingly not harming his driver. His loss was very keenly felt. Brigadier Hill said Juckes was "one of the finest junior leaders in the division." Major Roseveare later described the event as a tragedy in many words, but in his war diary back at the Ecarde quarry he made the normal brief logbook entry, "June 28th 1944 ... Usual mortar and shell fire. Captain T. R. Juckes killed."

It was from the Ecarde quarry that we saw the first massive raid on the city of Caen by some five hundred Allied bombers. It took place one fine evening (July 7th) and they came in from the sea, passing nearly directly overhead. Every man in the quarry climbed the perimeter walls seeking a good vantage point. Small patches of grey smoke were appearing by the score, and then by the hundred as the enemy brought every ack-ack gun to bear. We all stared in fascination at those hundreds of planes, maybe five thousand feet up, glinting in the sun as they made some minor change in course. One bomber started to descend, following a spiral course, and we could soon see that one wing was severely damaged. The lower it flew the more the ack-ack centred on it until it disappeared from our line of vision south west of the Orne. There was dismay written on every face. The bombing continued into the darkness when the flares and bomb flashes illuminated the vast pall of billowing smoke rising from Caen.

I was talking once with a Lance Corporal Windeatt, when we saw a stray horse that was grazing at the edge of the cliff bordering the quarry. We approached and eventually mounted it and went for a trot in the lanes nearby. Shortly afterwards, Jerry dropped flares over the quarry at night, and started dropping anti-personnel bombs and incendiary bombs. Most of us kept our heads down, apart from a few brave souls who dashed about putting out incendiaries. Some got burned with the phosphorus. There was also plenty of ack-ack fire, but no planes were brought down. By the time this raid occurred we had managed to build some really elaborate trenches, with a layer of rubble supported by scrap timber covering them, and we made good use of them that night.

The following morning a large audience was looking at a dead horse lying over the entrance to a trench. It was our stray horse, which had been hit by shrapnel before bolting over the quarry edge to die sprawled over the trench, occupied by Sergeant Poole. The sergeant was well liked, but we couldn't help laughing and letting him stew a while, in spite of his cries for help, before dragging off the poor horse and letting a spluttering sergeant come out.

One of the sappers, called Galletly, went to see the Medical Officer to get attention for a badly bruised arm. He returned with the arm in a sling and went into his dugout to make his bed. When sorting his blankets he found a half-buried unexploded bomb, and only then did he notice the damage to the layer of rubble and timber covering his dugout. "There was so much noise going on last night," he said, "I didn't realize there was a bomb in there with me!"

Attempts to invent ways of providing lighting in the dugouts were not very successful, the best probably being a cigarette tin of sand containing a drop of petrol. And we had one dugout job to do that few enjoyed, although it did not prove to be dangerous. General Gale administered the 6th Division from a chateau. It was damaged so often by enemy action that a large shelter, really an underground office, was designed, and a team of 3rd Squadron sappers chosen to dig it (July 20th). Whether this HQ dugout was for General Gale or

Brigadier Hill, or both, I really can't remember, but I was one of the RE team. We were split into shifts and worked at it. It was all in brown clay, which wasn't too bad, but twenty-seven feet long by seventeen feet wide by seven feet deep, which wasn't too good. It was all pick and shovel work and I thought we would never finish. It was completed by bridging the top with timber supporting a layer of the same clay, with a layer of rubble over that. Then ground water seeped in to a depth of two feet, so a noisy pump had to be installed to keep the water down, and a timber floor constructed, limiting the headroom. Not a happy project.

Shortly after this (July 26th) we received a visit from Field Marshal Montgomery who presented medal ribbons. Our 3rd Squadron commanding officer (Major Roseveare) was awarded the Distinguished Service Order. The Military Cross was awarded posthumously to Captain Juckes.

Major Roseveare's citation: *For conspicuous gallantry and devotion to duty. On the night of the 5th/6th June 1944, Major J. C. A. Roseveare was given the task of blowing up an important bridge at Troarn. He was dropped some five miles from his covering force, but he immediately gathered together a small force of Royal Engineers and some transport and made for his objective. Troarn was held by the enemy, but showing total disregard for his own safety and magnificent leadership he pushed his way through under heavy enemy fire and captured the bridge which he then successfully blew.*

Captain Juckes citation: *From the time he was dropped near Ranville on the night 5th/6th June until 1800 hours 8th June when his Troop was relieved in their defensive position, this officer has displayed the very highest powers of leadership, initiative and personal courage. He has been continually engaged in the execution of RE tasks in the face of the enemy and has led his Troop in an infantry role in a most aggressive fashion. After completing the demolition of two bridges at Bures he led a party including a platoon of 8th Para Battalion and forced a passage through Troarn, killing a number of Germans and taking prisoners, and carried out further demolitions on the partially demolished Troarn bridge. On withdrawing to the Brigade area at Le Mesnil his Troop occupied defensive positions for 30 hours, inflicting heavy casualties on the enemy. During this time he supervised the laying of an anti-tank minefield under fire. Throughout the whole of this time he lost no opportunity in harassing the enemy. This officer set a magnificent example to his junior officers and men by his tireless energy, enthusiasm and offensive eagerness.*

Later, Lieutenants Shave and Wade would also receive the Military Cross (MC), and Sergeant Shrubsole the Military Medal, for their actions at the Bures and Troarn bridges and in the subsequent holding of Le Mesnil, including raids against the enemy, the taking of prisoners and the laying of anti-tank mines under fire. Lieutenant Lack would receive the MC for a particularly dangerous reconnoitre mission, under fire, at bridges across the River Touques that were defended by the retreating Germans in August.

We were soon embroiled in sapper duties again, but with the blessing that we could retreat afterward to a quarry that was free of mortar attacks. But not free from aircraft attacks. Although not as bad as the mortar attacks at places like Le Mesnil, we suffered a number of men wounded during these air raids, including some really seriously injured who required repatriation.

Someone came up with the excellent idea of establishing a school where all enemy equipment would be forwarded so that it could be shown to all our personnel. I visited it and was immediately co-opted to explain and demonstrate some of our own equipment to Allied soldiers. I was somewhat put out to be shown how a particular grenade was superior to our own, in that the pin could be more easily withdrawn and replaced (if need be) than the pin in our own Mills grenade. Our 3rd Parachute Squadron officer, Lieutenant Lack, was demonstrating a German Panzerfaust anti-tank weapon, which I thought was very cleverly designed and easily operated. The business end was a shaped charge, similar to our beehive, this being attached to a piece of turned wood that was in turn housed in a snug fitting tube, also containing an explosive propellant. The operator simply tucked the tube under one arm, pointed the charge at a tank, and pressed a button that detonated the propellant explosive. This resulted in the charge flying towards the tank while the expended gasses from the explosive shot to the rear of the operator. The charge followed a satisfactory flight because thin steel vanes wrapped around the wood sprang out and guided the projectile as soon as it left the tube.

Lieutenant Lack demonstrated a Panzerfaust ('tank-fist') to every visiting group by blasting a new hole in a masonry wall, each hole big enough to drive a motorcycle through it. I for one found its simplicity and effectiveness most impressive. But they could be dangerous too. During one demonstration the lieutenant held the weapon a little too far forward, and the exploding propellant burned him badly by the right ribs, involving hospital treatment.

This 'demo' time was one of the more relaxing duties in which I was involved, and we also had opportunities to enjoy short breaks from the strain of dangerous work closer to the enemy. We were able to go for a swim in the Orne canal, where the banks were lined with scores of abandoned pleasure boats. We visited the coastal towns of Luc sur Mer, Lion sur Mer, and Ouistreham, and had the chance to examine the various Bailey bridges that had been erected by sea-borne sappers over the Orne river and Caen canal since D-Day. But our main quarters were at the Ecarde quarry, where life was fairly tolerable compared to spending time supporting the paratroop groups further east.

Our food was, for me, okay, being essentially compo rations (canned military composition foodstuffs designed to last a specific number of days) that were quite good. There were also some very nourishing biscuits, especially nice because the despatch riders were obliging at almost any time to get me a box of Camembert cheese. I think it was six weeks before bread replaced the biscuits, and I for one was sorry to see the biscuit ration stop, because by then I was used to their flavour, and the bread tasted like cotton wool. We were paid in small bank notes issued by the Allies, and honoured by them, each note bearing the tricolour of France.

I scrounged a ride on a truck going to the beach for rations, and was able to see the activity necessary to support the forward troops. At the beach I jumped on an amphibian craft, a DUKW or 'duck', and went out into the harbour sheltered by deliberately sunken ships. The RASC driver was no waterman, and waited for his turn to go alongside by aligning his wheeled and flat-bottomed craft broadside to the waves, which did my stomach no good at all. When he was eventually called alongside, I grabbed the hook of the ship's crane and was swung in a rather hair-raising loop on to the deck of the ship. After failing to scrounge a 'tea and a wad' (cup of tea and NAAFI sandwich) from the RE stevedores, I experienced an even more hair-raising return to the 'duck'. I jumped on top of a net full of ration boxes and held on to the hook while the crane driver lowered the load, which arrived just as a wave lifted the 'duck' about six feet. The net flipped off the hook and the ration boxes scattered, me included. Several boxes were lost overboard and I was lucky not to join them. Another few netfulls and the 'duck' headed for shore where it ran through the surf crabwise. Disembarking, I saluted a Naval beach master who grinned at me. A nice half-day out and break from the sapper work. Another time I visited a barber's shop, where a French girl in a spotless white uniform asked if I required a shampoo. Of course I did! But I was aghast to see the brown sludge running into the basin and made my apologies. I should have washed my hair in the canal before going there. But she made nothing of it, probably being used to soldiers in so unkempt a state.

Meanwhile the sapper jobs went on unremittingly. Replacement people came in from England, and one day I suddenly realized that there were only 27 year-old Corporal Rowbotham and myself remaining of all the original junior NCOs! One morning Sergeant Docherty grabbed Rowbotham and me and said, "I want someone for a job." This was nothing new, so we just grinned, and Rowbotham dug his hand into his pocket for a coin and said, "Toss you for it, Harry." He tossed, I called and won, and off he went.

I thought nothing more of it, but only an hour went by before someone arriving back from enemy shelling at Le Mesnil announced, "Corporal Rowbotham has just had it." There were about six people at his funeral, the first I had attended. He had been wrapped in a blanket and was lowered into the grave. An army padre read the service. I was in a daze, and just couldn't believe it. I could still see him quite vividly, his mass of dark freckles against a very white skin, his dark brown eyes, and chuckling as he said, in his slight north country accent, "Toss you for it, Harry."

Major Roseveare entered it concisely in his logbook, "29th July 1944 ... Tp (troop) rest day and baths ... Cpl Rowbotham killed by shellfire."

On a lighter note, and to lighten up, we sometimes sang a song about saving a world of supposedly social equality:

"The colonel kicked the major,
The major had a go,
He kicked the sergeant major,
Who kicked the NCO,
And as the kicks grew harder,
The corporal you can see,
Got kicked the way to bloody 'ell
To save democracy!"

It was usually very boring in the area when we were off duty, and most chaps rallied around to perform whenever an informal concert party was organized. Old jokes were polished, revised and extended. The audience was generally enthusiastic and generous in its praise. Old favourites were welcomed. These would include, "They're Digging Up Father's Grave To Build A Sewer", "The CRE" (Corps of Royal Engineers), "Don't you ever Cry", and a number of jokes and monologues that were pretty crude. There were usually two or three officers in the audience, they being bored too.

Between mid-August and the beginning of September we left our patch of ground between the River Dives and the River Orne and took part in a running battle with the retreating enemy. That was a pretty hazardous experience too, the German soldier being a very tough and efficient fighter. All sorts of memories crowd in when I think of that time, such as when I was walking along and a jeep stopped because the driver wanted to say something, but he didn't begin.

Mortar bombs started falling and he was really scared - not that I wasn't! His vehicle was full of boxes of ammunition that he was delivering, and we had visions of going up in a very big bang.

We were advancing along a road near Dives sur Mer, with our chaps mortaring from a position to our right front, and the enemy mortaring from a position beyond that. Jerry kept pulling back as we were hitting harder, but for all that he wasn't going away easily. Shortly after that we came upon a crossroads with freshly dug holes at the edges of the road. The holes were filled with huge artillery shells, each shell being three feet long and eight inches in diameter. The wires leading from them through several roadside fields were inspected but they were just loose on the ground, unconnected. Our route here had taken us through the remains of the city of Caen, and it was a very sobering sight that we had viewed from our vehicles as we followed bulldozed tracks through the mounds of masonry and the shells of ruined buildings.

Coming upon a village, we saw there were several buildings on fire, so we set to with buckets, doing the best we could. The volunteer fire brigade was frantic with frustration because the retreating Germans had deliberately sabotaged pumps and engine fittings before setting fire to the dwellings. At one hilltop where we paused, we were shelled by at least one 88mm gun. Someone recognized the distant rumble, the whine of the approaching shell and the sharp wham as it exploded. The only man near me with a sizeable slit trench was a wireless operator who was most reluctant to share it, but he had no option. 88mm shells were all going off in a piece of ground less than a hundred yards across, and each one blasted off shrapnel and left only a haze of thin blue smoke. It was a dreadful weapon, and produced nothing like the enormous billowing clouds created by a Hollywood movie shell.

We in 3rd Parachute Squadron were keeping well up front with the infantry as they struggled on, and in some villages and towns we were the first of the invasion forces that the residents had seen - so cheering, embracing and sometimes kissing were enthusiastic. Bottles and glasses suddenly materialized and there were lots of toasts and speeches, with little understanding but plenty of noisy goodwill. On one such occasion the rapidly appearing bottles still had earth sticking to them, from where they had been buried in hiding.

At one point the main road had been cratered very effectively where it had passed across a deep valley. The hollow depression in the embankment could easily have held three London buses. An army bulldozer was busy at work, flattening the lip of the crater to create a makeshift road around half of its perimeter. Nearby were three new graves marked with stakes, and on the middle one there was a German Officer's hat. Being conscious of booby traps, no one would go near them. Three members of the Maquis (French Resistance fighters who harassed the Germans and helped the Allies, especially during the Normandy invasion) came to greet us from the east side of the crater, carrying rifles on their shoulders and each wearing an armband bearing the cross of Alsace Lorraine. I was the only soldier with enough French to converse with them, and they soon explained that they had shot the three Germans and buried them there. It seemed that the Germans had been doing a reconnoitre job, because later a follow-up group of German engineers arrived and cratered the road. After exchanging news and pleasantries, they departed. Now knowing that it was safe, I immediately walked over to the graves and grabbed the hat, much to the chagrin of the others and the bulldozer operator whom I had beaten to the prize. The white piping around the brim and the style of silver braid on the hat meant that the late owner had been an infantry field officer.

It took us about two weeks to reach Honfleur, the small port on the south side of the River Seine estuary. In the town there were joyful celebrations, and there were also old scores being settled. French collaborators and any who had been seen cooperating with the Germans were being punished, including a number of women who were forcibly having their heads shaved, a public mark of shame. I saw a crowd around a woman with her head freshly shaven, but hadn't the stomach to watch any more and left the scene. Our Squadron was billeted in and around a chateau, and it was from here that we would begin our journey home.

And so this task ended for the 3rd Parachute Squadron RE and we made our final departure on September 6th, bound for England after having served in France for ninety-one days. Our exit was not far from where we had arrived, on the coast of Normandy, just some twenty miles northwest of Caen at Arromanches beach. There we boarded HMS Empire Gauntlet in Mulberry harbour 'B', one of two temporary docking facilities that had been pre-fabricated and floated across the English Channel in Operation Neptune with the invading D-Day army.

Our role as airborne troops had always been explained to us as one where we went in first, held a position while the main body of troops came in, by land or sea, and took over from us, while we returned to re-equip and re-train for the next operation. So what we had experienced was a long tough operation rather than a short tough operation. Not that we were complaining. We simply assumed that it had taken a fair bit longer than the planners had estimated.

We felt the loss of a lot of good men very acutely, most of them being buried back in Ranville, about one mile west of Le Mesnil, a cemetery of nearly all 6th Airborne Division graves. And we carried with us some terrible memories. Mortar and shellfire had been the end of every original junior NCO in the squadron - except me. So many sappers who had flown in on D-Day had been killed or wounded. But we also felt that by completing our demolition tasks we had enabled the Division to hold the eastern bridgehead until reinforcements arrived, followed by breakout and driving back the enemy. We could be proud of the part we had played. We thought that we would probably get some leave, and then more training, and meanwhile we could think about what the next task might be.

THE LIBERATION OF NORWAY · 8th MAY 1945

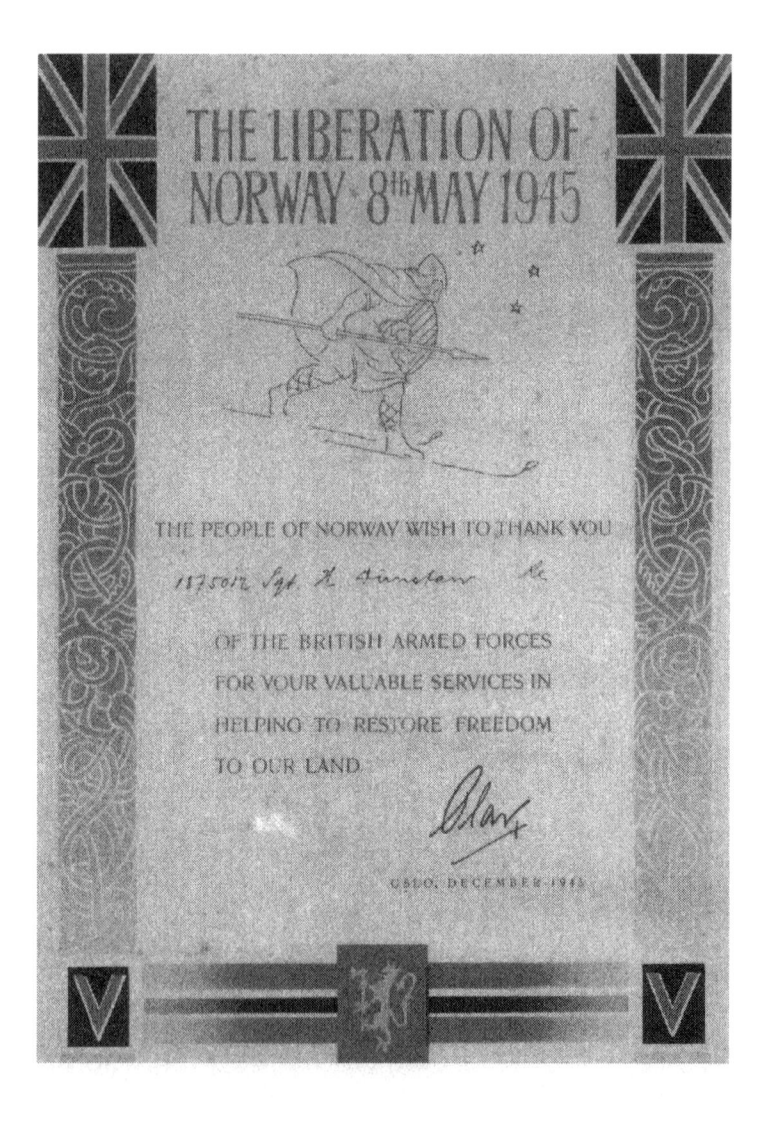

THE PEOPLE OF NORWAY WISH TO THANK YOU

1875012 Sgt. H. Dunstow

OF THE BRITISH ARMED FORCES
FOR YOUR VALUABLE SERVICES IN
HELPING TO RESTORE FREEDOM
TO OUR LAND

Olav

OSLO, DECEMBER 1945

RAS EL EIN VILLAGE - PALESTINE - NOV. 1945.

AIRBORNE
British Insignia (Pegasus)
For additional data and an official record see:
The War Diary of the 3rd Parachute Squadron RE in Normandy
signed by CO Major Roseveare (National Archives WO 171/1510)
http://www.pegasusarchive.org/normandy/war_3parasqn.htm

About The Engineer

Harry Ivor Dunstan was born in 1920 in Camborne, Cornwall, England, which along with the twin town of Redruth was once center of a very prosperous tin-mining industry. The family farmhouse in which Harry grew up was surrounded by old mineshafts, and the farm was called 'Tolcarne', literally meaning 'the hole in the hill'. Harry attended Redruth Grammar School before being sent to the army Technical School at Beachley, Chepstow, from 1935 until 1938. His WW2 service years as described in this book spanned from 1939 to 1944.

At the end of the War in Europe, 1st and 6th Airborne paratroops were part of Operation Doomsday, the liberation of Nazi-occupied Norway in 1945, facilitating the enemy surrender and clearing the ground of hazards such as mines. Harry was among the Royal Engineers engaged in this task. The 6th Airborne Division also became involved in tense peacekeeping duties in Israel. The British military directive (from 1945-48) was to prevent bloodshed between Arabs and zealous adherents to the newly emerging Jewish State, to police the area without becoming embroiled in counter-violence. In 1945, Harry was briefly involved in this general mandate, and even personally sent in pursuit of an escaped Arab murderer across the desert near Beersheba. Chasing the fugitive by jeep, he eventually shot the fleeing man in the leg in order to bring him back to Jerusalem, to face his tribe, his Sheik, and justice.

Upon returning to civilian life, Harry studied at the world-renowned Camborne School of Mines, from 1946-49, and qualified as a mining engineer, the only graduate to score 100% in all 12 rigorous subjects. For this he was awarded a short-term scholarship to study ore production in the gold mines at Timmins, Ontario, in Canada. On his return to England, he applied to the government (as was required after the war for people with skills considered to be of national value) for permission to work with the company of John Taylor & Sons in Kolar Gold Fields, a small township in southern India that was then the country's main producer of gold. He worked there as supervisor of an underground mine (2 miles deep!) from 1949-1955.

As political change and nationalisation of the mines became imminent in India, Harry returned to England. For 2 years he worked with English China Clays (ECC), in Cornwall, as an area mine manager, before he was selected in 1957 to be a mines superintendent for Alcan (Aluminum of Canada) in Jamaica. After almost 12 years in the West Indies, he again returned to Cornwall and to ECC in 1968, where he worked in the Overseas Department, newly created to explore for all forms of calcium carbonate similar to kaolin (china clay).

This took him to investigate potential ores in Australia (clay), South Africa (clay), Italy (marble), Brazil (clay), Greece (magnesite), Belgium (chalk), and once again to northern France (chalk), where he came across trenches that he had dug long ago in WW2, and met people in farmhouses that remembered him as a soldier.

He retired from ECC in 1980, in the small Cornish coastal village of Mevagissey. He had many hobbies before and after retirement, and was an accomplished artist in oils, watercolours, and pastels. A craftsman in metallurgy and woodwork, his great love was sailboats. In Jamaica he undertook the construction of two yachts, 30 and 32 feet long, and finally in Cornwall a 38-foot ketch. These he built single-handed, from keel construction to steam bending the ribs, converting bus diesel engines for seawater service, and sewing sails on a vintage foot-treadle Singer machine salvaged from a town dump in Belgium where he was looking for mine ores.

Harry passed away in 2004, after exactly 60 years of marriage to his wife Margie, whom he met and married during WW2. They now both rest in Trewinney Cemetery at the top of School Hill in Mevagissey, Cornwall.

Printed in Poland
by Amazon Fulfillment
Poland Sp. z o.o., Wrocław